Funding and the Quest for Sovereignty in Palestine

Anas Iqtait

# Funding and the Quest for Sovereignty in Palestine

palgrave
macmillan

Anas Iqtait
Braddon, ACT, Australia

ISBN 978-3-031-19477-1    ISBN 978-3-031-19478-8 (eBook)
https://doi.org/10.1007/978-3-031-19478-8

© The Author(s), under exclusive license to Springer Nature Switzerland AG 2023
This work is subject to copyright. All rights are solely and exclusively licensed by the Publisher, whether the whole or part of the material is concerned, specifically the rights of translation, reprinting, reuse of illustrations, recitation, broadcasting, reproduction on microfilms or in any other physical way, and transmission or information storage and retrieval, electronic adaptation, computer software, or by similar or dissimilar methodology now known or hereafter developed.
The use of general descriptive names, registered names, trademarks, service marks, etc. in this publication does not imply, even in the absence of a specific statement, that such names are exempt from the relevant protective laws and regulations and therefore free for general use.
The publisher, the authors, and the editors are safe to assume that the advice and information in this book are believed to be true and accurate at the date of publication. Neither the publisher nor the authors or the editors give a warranty, expressed or implied, with respect to the material contained herein or for any errors or omissions that may have been made. The publisher remains neutral with regard to jurisdictional claims in published maps and institutional affiliations.

Cover illustration: © John Rawsterne/patternhead.com

This Palgrave Macmillan imprint is published by the registered company Springer Nature Switzerland AG
The registered company address is: Gewerbestrasse 11, 6330 Cham, Switzerland

*I dictate this book to my family in Palestine. My parents, Abeer and Ibrahim, have always been behind me in every way, inspiring me to go further at every step, and this last achievement has been no exception. Without their care and support, my current professional and academic achievements would have been unthinkable.*

*I also cannot praise enough my wife and most esteemed colleague, Azima Akhmatova. She has inspired and guided me at every turn. I owe the completeness of this research to her endless love and encouragement. I dedicate this book to her and to our son, Obaida.*

*Finally, to the steadfast people of Palestine, I dedicate this book.*

# FOREWORD

Over US$45 billion has been spent since 1993 by international donors as aid for Palestinians living in the occupied West Bank and Gaza Strip. This makes Palestinians one of the highest per capita recipients of non-military aid in the world. Inspite of those sums, however, peace and development remain elusive, and this aid has failed to achieve its three main objectives: lasting peace, effective and accountable Palestinian institutions and sustainable socioeconomic development. Due to the aid modality and structures dictated by the Oslo Accords framework, Palestinians are therefore forced to live in an aid-development paradox and in an entrenched status of dependency and reliance on that aid.

Furthermore, the economic framework of Oslo Accords, imposed an arrangement on the Palestinians whereby Israel, the occupying power, controls, inter alia, the process of collecting the majority of indirect taxes on behalf of the Palestinian Authority (PA) under the so-called clearance revenue mechanism. Accordingly, about 70 per cent of the PA's domestic revenue is collected, processed and transferred (or not) by Israel to the PA on a monthly basis.

These figures on foreign aid and indirect taxes collected by Israel are problematic, and they illustrate the wider context of control and dependency. They also explain some of the root causes for the denial of development in Palestine and the perpetuation of cycles of de-development. Hence, it is vital to understand the processes that lead to such dependency and the factors that have sustained them over the past three decades. It is

viii FOREWORD

also equally important to better understand and analyse the consequences and ramifications of relying on public revenues that are not under the control of the governing body, the PA, and how the broader elements of statehood and sovereignty are impacted by the persistence of such dynamics.

Against this backdrop, this book, *Funding and the Quest for Sovereignty in Palestine* by Dr. Anas Iqtait, explores, examines and problematises the political economy of public revenues in Palestine—particularly since the establishment of the PA in 1993/94—through the lens of fiscal sociology. It argues that without sovereignty or control over border crossings, the PA remains dependent on two sources of income, namely, foreign aid and Israeli-controlled and processed clearance revenue. Those two sources of revenues are fully controlled by external actors, foreign donors and Israel. Stripping the PA from any control over these two resources was not accidental or unintentional. It was part and parcel of the Oslo Accords arrangements and conditionality, which aimed to create an inflated dependent national bureaucracy that is unable to and incapable of leading the Palestinians into sovereignty, statehood, self-determination or freedom.

Therefore, and due to the design of the Oslo Accords and the power imbalances associated with it, the PA emerged as an institution that is largely accountable to the 'external rent providers', the donors and Israel, instead of being accountable to the Palestinian people, which in turn hindered its local legitimacy. To illustrate the magnitude of the issue, and encapsulate it in one figure, between 1997 and 2020, about 76 per cent of the PA's revenues derived from sources of revenue controlled by external actors. Additionally, the Palestinian economy is rent-driven, with a rent-to-GDP ratio of 37 per cent, as explored in the third chapter of this book.

These lines of argumentation are eloquently explored and investigated by Dr. Anas Iqtait in this book through the original analytical lens of fiscal sociology. This approach did not only allow Dr. Iqtait to advance a theoretical framework of 'dual rentierism'; it also permitted Dr. Iqtait to study the effects of this dual rentierism framework on the economic structure, tax collection, economic planning and fiscal policy. And therefore, this book explores how dual rentierism shaped the formation of PA–society relations. In other words, it examines how the architecture of fiscal control and the PA's dual rentierism hindered and distorted the process of establishing a social contract with Palestinians in the occupied West Bank and Gaza Strip.

Instead of investing in building a social contract that matters to a liberation movement, the PA leadership adopted 'internationally pleasing and acceptable' paradigms, instead of being locally rooted and oriented. In other words, international legitimacy suppressed local legitimacy. This in turn, and as explained in the fifth chapter of this book, meant that the PA–society relations is characterised by the dominance of authoritarianism, absence of effective and representative political institutions and leadership, multi-headed fragmentations and deep mistrust and endemic corruption. Looking at these factors through the lens of fiscal sociology, as Dr. Iqtait offers in this important and remarkable book, shed new light on insights that problematises the critical role of public revenues and public institutions vis-à-vis local legitimacy, accountability of governance structures and effectiveness of the political systems.

As we presented in *Political Economy of Palestine: Critical, Interdisciplinary, and Decolonial Perspectives* (Palgrave Macmillan, 2021), political economy is concerned with institutions, relations of power and social contract, conflict and struggle. A key task of a political economy framework is to historicise and (re)politicise economics, and to unveil critical elements of both the material and discursive expressions of power. Therefore, a political economy approach also underscores that an approach to economics that does not consider the political—a depoliticised economics—is inadequate to understanding the situation in occupied Palestine. *Funding and the Quest for Sovereignty in Palestine* by Dr. Iqtait is a valuable, distinctive and original contribution to this body of literature that aims to emphasise and underscore the importance of political economy framework to better explain and analyse the complex relationship between public revenues and the quest for sovereignty and statehood in Palestine. If anything, this book coherently and convincingly shows that it is not surprising that thirty years after Oslo Accords, Palestinians have emerged weaker, more fragmented and further away from statehood.

October 2022

Dr. Alaa Tartir
Senior Researcher
The Geneva Graduate Institute
Geneva, Switzerland

**Dr. Alaa Tartir** is a Senior Researcher and Academic Coordinator at the Geneva Graduate Institute, a Global Fellow at the Peace Research Institute Oslo (PRIO), and a Policy and Program Advisor to Al- Shabaka: The Palestinian Policy Network. He is the co-editor of *Political Economy of Palestine: Critical, Interdisciplinary, and Decolonial Perspectives* (Palgrave Macmillan, 2021) and *Palestine and Rule of Power: Local Dissent vs. International Governance* (Palgrave Macmillan, 2019). Tartir can be followed on Twitter (@alaatartir), and his publications can be accessed at www.alaatartir.com.

# CONTENTS

| | | |
|---|---|---|
| 1 | Introduction | 1 |
| 2 | Fiscal Sociology, Political Rents, and Dual Rentierism | 15 |
| 3 | Fiscal and Economic History of the West Bank and Gaza Strip | 37 |
| 4 | The Palestinian Authority's Economy of Dual Rentierism | 71 |
| 5 | The Societal Legacy of Dual Rentierism | 97 |
| 6 | Rents, Revenue, and Sovereignty | 141 |
| | Index | 151 |

# ABBREVIATIONS

| | |
|---|---|
| AMAN | Coalition for Accountability and Integrity |
| ASYCUDA | Automated System for Customs Data Analysis |
| EEC | European Economic Community |
| GDI | Gross Disposable Income |
| GDP | Gross Domestic Product |
| GNI | Gross National Income |
| GNP | Gross National Product |
| GUPT | General Union of Palestinian Teachers |
| GUPTOT | General Union for Palestinian Teachers in the Occupied Territories |
| ICBS | Israeli Central Bureau of Statistics |
| IMF | International Monetary Fund |
| MEHE | Ministry of Education and Higher Education |
| MoFP | Ministry of Finance and Planning |
| NDC | NGO Development Center |
| NGO | Non-Governmental Organisations |
| NPISH | Non-Profit Institutions Serving Households |
| PA | Palestinian Authority |
| PCBS | Palestinian Central Bureau of Statistics |
| PECDAR | Palestinian Economic Council for Development and Reconstruction |
| PLO | Palestinian Liberation Organisation |
| PNGO | Palestinian Non-Governmental Organisations Network |
| RST | Rentier State Theory |
| UNDP | United Nationals Development Programme |
| UNESCO | United Nations Educational, Scientific and Cultural Organization |

xiii

xiv  ABBREVIATIONS

UNRWA    United Nations Relief and Works Agency for Palestine Refugees in
         the Near East
USAID    United States Agency for International Development

# List of Figures

Fig. 1.1  Foreign aid disbursement in Palestine, 1997–2019. Based on data from World Bank and IMF publications 1997–2019 — 5

Fig. 1.2  PA revenues: foreign aid, clearance revenue, and local revenue, 1997–2020. Based on data from World Bank and IMF publications 1997–2021 — 6

Fig. 3.1  Percentage of Palestinian labour force employed in Israel, 1970–1993 (Calculated from ICBS [1996] data) — 42

Fig. 3.2  Remittances flow to Palestinian economy (current USD and relative to GDP), 1995–2020 (Calculated from data by World Bank [n.d.(b)]) — 48

Fig. 3.3  Percentage of Palestinian labour force employed in Israel, 1970–2020 (*Source* Author's calculations from ICBS [1996] and PCBS [n.d.(a)] data) — 49

Fig. 3.4  Percentage of unemployment in Palestine, 1994–2019 (*Source* Author's calculations from World Bank [n.d.(b)] data) — 51

Fig. 3.5  Labour force distribution in Palestine, 1994–2020 (Calculated from PCBS [n.d.(a)] data) — 51

Fig. 3.6  Rentier income (remittances and foreign aid) as per cent of GDP, 1995–2019 (Calculated from World Bank [n.d.(b)] data) — 52

Fig. 3.7  PA revenue in 2020 (Calculated from data in the Palestinian Ministry of Finance and Planning Quarterly Budgetary Reports 2020) — 58

xv

| | | |
|---|---|---|
| Fig. 4.1 | Clearance revenue composition, 2008–2021 (*Source* Calculated from data in the Ministry of Finance and Planning Monthly Budgetary Report, 2008–2021) | 83 |
| Fig. 4.2 | The Palestinian Authority's rentier trap (*Source* Author's analysis) | 90 |
| Fig. 5.1 | PA employees and public sector as percentage of total labour force, 1994–2020 (*Source* Calculated from Palestinian Central Bureau of Statistics data) | 112 |
| Fig. 5.2 | The rentier triangle of reliance (*Source* Author analysis) | 128 |

# LIST OF TABLES

| | | |
|---|---|---|
| Table 3.1 | Public expenditures and revenues in the West Bank and Gaza, 1968–1993 (million New Israeli Shekel [ILS], 1986 prices) | 45 |
| Table 3.2 | PA fiscal operations, 1994–2020 (current USD millions) | 54 |
| Table 3.3 | History of clearance revenue transfer suspensions | 60 |
| Table 4.1 | Palestinian traders' interaction with Israel and PA | 84 |

CHAPTER 1

# Introduction

**Abstract** This chapter outlines the main argument of the book: that decades of external economic development programs and Israeli economic policies have left the Palestinian Authority doubly dependent on external income in the form of foreign aid and clearance revenue. This dependence, and the technical and political conditionalities for disbursement of that income, has altered the accountability of the PA in favour of rent providers and hampered the Palestinian quest for statehood.

**Keywords** Fiscal sociology · External income · Foreign aid · Clearance revenue · Palestinian Authority · Dual rentierism

The question of how revenues shape the formation and behaviour of states has long been a pertinent one. Joseph Schumpeter was among the first to highlight the centrality of revenue and taxation to the state, observing that 'the extraction of tax revenue by the state has an enormous influence on economic organization, social structure, human spirit and culture, and the fate of nations' (Campbell 1993, p. 163). He further asserted 'that the study of the social processes behind taxation and public finances, that is, fiscal sociology, is one of the best starting points for an investigation of society, and particularly its political life' (Campbell 1993, p. 163). For Schumpeter, fiscal sociology goes beyond superficial facts of

© The Author(s), under exclusive license to Springer Nature Switzerland AG 2023
A. Iqtait, *Funding and the Quest for Sovereignty in Palestine*, https://doi.org/10.1007/978-3-031-19478-8_1

1

budgetary data to examine the nexus between contemporary and historical fiscal affairs and social and economic structures (Musgrave 1992). Schumpeter's intellectual contemporary in the early twentieth century, Rudolf Goldscheid, argued further that the 'pattern of public finance has at all times had a decisive influence on national and social evolution. Tax struggles were the oldest form of class struggle, and fiscal matters were an important contributory cause even in the mightiest spiritual movements of mankind' (Goldscheid 1958, p. 202).

However, it was Max Weber's conception of the modern state, not those of Schumpeter or Goldscheid, that largely shaped scholarly understandings of the state's formation and behaviour. Weber attributed the emergence of the modern European representative state to the rise of modern rational bureaucracy (Weber 1978). In doing so, he emphasised the state's 'organizational means' over the 'functions it performed or the motives that drove state elites' (Moore 2001, p. 399). For Schumpeter, Weber's approach resulted in oversimplification of the role revenues play in determining state policies. Schumpeter argued that the expansion of the 'tax apparatus' into the economy has monumental ramifications, shaping the rise of a system of 'binding constraints on governments and institutionalized political representation that constitute the foundations of liberal democracy' (Moore 2004, p. 299). A nation's dependence on tax extraction, in contrast to other sources of revenue, for financing government activities forms a 'social contract' between the state and its populace (Ertman 1997; Levi 1999). In the tax state, 'economic institutions, political institutions, and social and cultural norms have all evolved in a way that supports a broad tax base and a reasonable degree of tax compliance. The demand for accountable and transparent government is fuelled by citizens who are aware of the need to ensure that tax revenues are wisely spent' (Besley and Persson 2014, p. 118). Thus, tax states are composed of institutional and political structures that allow states to bargain with their societies and citizens in order to collect taxes (Moore 2001, p. 404).

In recent years, fiscal sociology has gained traction in development and state-building literature, drawing attention to the instrumental role of the state's fiscal composition in the construction of state institutions and policies in developing countries. While previous literature on fiscal sociology has highlighted the dynamics of taxation in the formation of the Western European representative state, modern developing countries have access to other forms of state revenues, such as natural resources or political rents. Rentier income has been defined as 'income derived from [a] gift of nature', such as natural resources, or as 'unearned foreign income', such as remittances or foreign aid (Beblawi 1987, p. 49). There is a growing body of literature that assesses the effects of this rentier income, as opposed to fiscal extraction and taxation, on the construction and behaviour of the state (see, e.g., Bizhan 2018; Iqtait 2017, 2021). Rentier income is thought to produce particular political, economic and institutional outcomes and to alter state–society relations. States that rely on rents do not need to resort to collecting taxes from their populace in order to finance their expenditures. The absence, or weakness, of taxes and the tax apparatus in these states eliminates the need for representation and allows the state to remain autonomous of its citizens (Beblawi 1987, pp. 51–52). In other words, the state lacks a 'social contract' with its society. Thus, institutional and political structures that allow states to bargain with their societies and citizens are replaced by a 'rentier bargain', whereby states allocate material benefits in exchange for political quiescence (Beblawi 1987, pp. 51–52). These dynamics are described by a political economic theory, the *Rentier State Theory* (RST), which is about states that accrue most of their income from rentier income. These rents include natural resource rents, location rents, political rents and remittances (Richter and Steiner 2008; Jenkins et al. 2011; Moore 2004). Chapter 2 provides a critical overview of the evolution of the study of public revenues in fiscally dependent states.

Foreign aid is one of the most abundant forms of external income, also described as political rents. Access to such aid has been sought for decades for achieving different political, development, strategic or humanitarian objectives. Foreign aid is defined as an external transfer of capital or resources from one country (the donor) to another (the recipient) (Abbott 1970). It takes several forms, ranging from technical assistance and knowledge transformation to fixed capital delivery and financial support. Foreign aid objectives have evolved to address specific gaps viewed as significant at a particular point in time. For example, in the 1950s the focus was infrastructure and technical skills construction (as in the Marshall Plan); in the 1980s it was promoting productive economic growth; in the 1990s the gap was human rights, good governance and democracy promotion; and, most recently, aid has been dedicated to the achievement of the United Nations' Millennium Development Goals and internationally led state-building initiatives (Riddell 2008). Before the recent downscaling of global aid levels, previous decades had witnessed a surge in foreign aid flows (Rad 2015). This surge in aid flows was associated with a broader international trend whereby institution- and state-building developed into an integral part of conflict resolution and peacekeeping in conflict and post-conflict countries (Fukuyama 2007). Examples of this trend include the large disbursements of foreign aid to international state-building efforts in Afghanistan, East Timor, Iraq, Kosovo and Palestine.

Foreign aid played a central role in the establishment and formation of the Palestinian Authority (PA) since 1994, and has continued to represent a noticeable percentage of the PA's budget as well as that of the overall Palestinian economy. Taking into account the small geographical area and low population of the West Bank and Gaza, foreign aid to the Palestinians can be described as one of the largest internationally funded projects since the Second World War (Brynen 2000). Between 1994 and 2019, Palestinians in the West Bank and Gaza received more than USD 41 billion in foreign aid, putting them among the highest aid per capita recipients in the world. Palestinians were, for example, some of the highest foreign aid recipients per capita in the world in 2019, with USD 423 per capita— significantly higher than the average per capita foreign aid received in the Middle East and North Africa region (USD 60), fragile and conflict-affected areas (USD 65) or the world average (USD 25) (World Bank 2021).

Foreign aid in Palestine is broadly divided into two categories according to disbursement: PA budgetary support, and all other forms of humanitarian and development aid. PA budgetary support represents foreign aid that donors channel through the PA's budget, which includes recurrent and development expenditures. In addition to this, other forms of humanitarian and development aid are disbursed through a variety of Palestinian or international organisations such as local and international non-governmental organisations (NGOs) and United Nations developmental and humanitarian agencies. As Fig. 1.1 highlights, budgetary support consumed 46 per cent of all foreign aid disbursed in Palestine between 1997 and 2019. These disbursements have represented 30 per cent of all public revenue available to the PA in the same period.

Foreign aid is not the only source of external income accruing to the PA, with Israeli-controlled clearance revenues also representing a substantial portion of the PA's budget. The PA's domestic fiscal operations are determined by the principles of the Paris Protocol, signed in 1994 by Israel and the Palestinian Liberation Organization (PLO) on behalf of the PA. The Protocol limited to a large extent the capacity

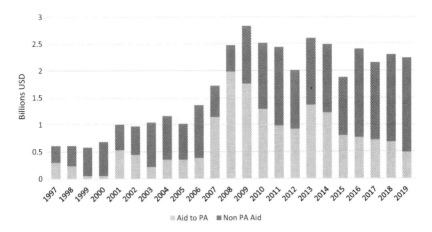

**Fig. 1.1** Foreign aid disbursement in Palestine, 1997–2019. Based on data from World Bank and IMF publications 1997–2019

of the PA to formulate its own trade and fiscal regimes. Because the PA lacked control over borders, the Protocol proposed a revenue clearance mechanism, under which Israel collects, processes and transfers to the PA taxes imposed on Palestinian international imports and exports, including those from Israel. The mechanism also accounts for income taxes from wages earned by Palestinian workers in Israel. The value of clearance revenue has grown consistently to the point that it represents the largest source of revenue for the PA, averaging 46 per cent of the PA's total public revenues. When omitting foreign aid disbursements in the form of budgetary support, clearance revenue accounts for 65 per cent of PA's available revenue. Figure 1.2 shows the relative composition of the PA's total revenues, which include the PA's clearance revenue, foreign aid in the form of budgetary support, and local tax and non-tax revenue. Between 1997 and 2020, about 76 per cent of the PA's revenues derive from sources of revenue controlled by external actors. On average, only 24 per cent of the PA's revenue lies under its full discretion (namely, income taxes, corporate taxes and other forms of non-tax revenues; Chapter 3 details the composition of the PA's revenue).

Although scholars have addressed the relationship between foreign aid and Palestinian state-building and Palestinian society, the dynamics of this relationship with regard to the PA's wider public revenues are little

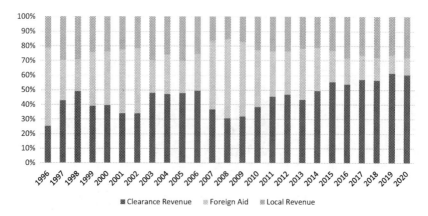

**Fig. 1.2** PA revenues: foreign aid, clearance revenue, and local revenue, 1997–2020. Based on data from World Bank and IMF publications 1997–2021

understood, and no in-depth examination of the PA's budget components has been conducted. This includes the effects of the PA's dependence on clearance revenue, the different effects of the foreign aid disbursed through the PA's budget versus that disbursed through projects bypassing the PA, and the role and prevalence of external income accruing to the wider Palestinian economy. Nor are there any recent studies examining the nexus between contemporary and historical fiscal affairs and the social and economic structures of the West Bank and Gaza. In other words, the fiscal sociology of the PA is still poorly understood.

Before exploring some of these issues, we should first clarify what we mean by the terms 'state' and 'state–society relations' in Palestine. Defining the state in Palestine can be addressed from two perspectives. The first studies the internationally led state-building efforts in establishing, designing and financing the Palestinian Authority since 1993. Bräutigam (2008, p. 2) defines state-building as 'the process of increasing the administrative, fiscal and institutional capacity of governments to interact constructively with their societies and to pursue public goals more effectively'. International state-building, however, is defined as 'an externally driven, or facilitated, attempt to form or consolidate a stable, and sometimes democratic, government' (Berger 2006, p. 6). Berger (2006) demarcates international state-building as encompassing peace-building, conflict resolution, national construction and foreign aid under the auspices of major international donors, such as the United States and European states, or international or regional organisations, such as the World Bank and the International Monetary Fund. The state-building process in Palestine has been fostered primarily by the World Bank and international donors, primarily the United States and European Union states, to create the Palestinian Authority. However, a significant divergence in this approach from the above definition is that the international state-building process of the PA was directed at the creation of a 'self-government entity' rather than a fully functional state (World Bank 1994, p. 1). The second perspective on defining the state in Palestine addresses the view of scholarly literature on the classification of the PA. Various writers have debated the contextual setting of the international state-building of the PA, arguing that this process contradicted the foundational premises of 'state-building', since the PA lacks sovereignty over territory (e.g., Kanafani 2011; Telhami 2001; Brown 2003; Lia 2006). Others question the internal course of the process, citing fragmentation, authoritarianism, neopatrimonialism and dependence (Brynen 1995; Tartir et al. 2013; Jarbawi and Pearlman 2007; Halper 2006). Ad-Duweik (2013) and Khalil (2013) classify the PA as a political system with partial sovereignty, exercising powers within a limited legal and constitutional framework. Al-Madbouh (2017) classifies the PA as a 'quasi-political system', arguing that the foundations of the political system in Palestine are troubled by a unique set of internal and external mechanisms, such as factional competition, Israeli occupation and aid dependency.

Against this backdrop, in focusing on the nature of the state in Palestine it is imperative to clarify that the PA, while not a state, is very much a governing authority (Jamal 2007; Brown 2003). Thus, although the PA is not a state, it will be treated as one for the purpose of analysis in this book. As Brown (2003, p. 144) explains: 'There is no doubt that the PA has exercised most state functions from the perspective of most [international] organizations, providing the legal framework and undertaking policing and licensing functions'. This conceptualisation is used in this book. By treating the PA as a state, the book is not attempting to downplay the overarching and prevalent role the Israeli occupation plays in the economic, political and societal space in Palestine. Nor does it underestimate the extensive influence of international actors such as the United States and European Union on Palestine and the PA. Rather, the purpose of this conceptualisation is to explore the ways in which the sources of revenue for the PA shape patterns of policy-making and state–society relations. In this regard, Hilal (2006) contextualises state–society relations in Palestine since the formation of the PA as comprising civil society organisations, labour unions, the business community and political factions. Since the PA is the central theme of research, this book juxtaposes the governing PA with Palestinian civil society organisations, labour unions and the business community as representatives of Palestinian society. In order to contextualise the Palestinian state–society relationship carefully, the Israeli occupation will be present in much of the analysis. However, this book is not about the relationship between Palestinian society and the Israeli occupation. Although this is a topic of great importance and significance, the lens in this book is focused on the context of the PA's relationship with the Palestinian economy and society, although as these relations are partly shaped by the ongoing Israeli occupation, the research unavoidably refers to this throughout.

This book explores—in both historical and contemporary terms—the political economy of public revenues in Palestine through the lens of fiscal sociology. In particular, it focuses on the drivers and constraints that have shaped the PA's policy development and state-building associated with its dependence on external income. The book demonstrates that decades of external economic development programs and Israeli economic policies have left the Palestinian economy doubly dependent on external income. Since the PA's inception in 1994, it has set up institutions that were intended to form the core of a future Palestinian state, involving the establishment of ministries and agencies, an extensive security apparatus and a tax system. However, without real sovereignty or control over border crossings, the PA remains dependent on two sources of income: foreign aid and Israeli-controlled and processed clearance revenue. It further argues that this dependence on external income—and the technical and political conditionalities for disbursement of that income—have altered the accountability of the PA in favour of rent providers. It elaborates on how the need for fiscal survivability has thwarted the Palestinian quest for statehood. The book advances a theoretical framework of dual rentierism, whereby the PA is dependent on two different types of external income. Through customising RST, the book adopts a critical political economy approach, making the case that external sources of PA income represent political rents that need to be disaggregated and studied concurrently.

This book contributes to the broader literature on Palestine studies and to area studies of the Middle East, and, specifically to furthering understanding of the Palestinian political economy. The book is the first of its kind to apply the RST framework to the PA's political economy. Although academics have undertaken numerous studies of international aid, economic relations with Israel, civil society, state formation and state-building, and the democratisation and securitisation of the PA, there have been no attempts to understand the effects of PA's revenues on its policy-making. By focusing on the PA's two main sources of revenue—foreign aid and clearance revenue—this book aims to shed light on the effects of the PA's rentierism on its policy-making. In addition, the application of RST has hitherto been limited largely to the understanding of natural resource rentier states. This book seeks to contribute to the RST literature in two ways. Firstly, it applies RST in a non-natural resource rentier context by suggesting a modified rentier framework based on political rentierism. Secondly, it utilises RST to explore the effects of two different sources of political rentier income on the PA. Thus, this book is the first of its kind to apply an RST framework to understand the impact of two sources of political rentier income on the recipient state. In doing so, the research is also the first to implement a fiscal sociological approach to the PA. Finally, given the persistent Israeli occupation of Palestine and repeated attempts at declaring a Palestinian state in the West Bank and Gaza, unravelling the dynamics of the PA's revenues arguably contributes to the understanding of any future Palestinian state. Thus, in addition to contributing to the academic literature on Palestine and the PA, in a practical sense, this book also aims to supply domestic and international policy-makers with a better conception of the fiscal viability and composition of a future Palestinian state.

In order to make sense of the politico-economy of external income and public revenue in Palestine since 1967, the book is divided into six chapters. Chapter 2 advances a theoretical framework for political rentierism, justifying the classification of PA's external income sources of foreign aid and clearance revenue as political rents. It will compare the characteristics of political rents and natural resource rents from the point of view of the accruing state and examine the effects of political rents on the economy, state–society relations and taxation. It will further theorise the concept of dual rentierism. Chapter 2 provides a detailed description of the theoretical framework upon which this research rests by introducing a modified RST framework of political rentierism. In doing so, it lists the varying sources of revenues available to states, such as taxes and rents in the form of oil revenue, remittances, foreign aid and other forms of political rents.

It introduces the rentier state and RST and illustrates the effects of rents on the economy and state–society relations. The chapter then examines how RST could be utilised to investigate the impacts of political rents, such as foreign aid and clearance revenue, in the Palestinian context. It does so by comparing the characteristics of political rents and natural resource rents, examining the effects of political rents on the economy, state–society relations, and taxation. Chapter 3 evaluates the presence and prevalence of rentier income in a historical context. It looks at how the Palestinian economy has evolved over two distinct periods. The first was the evolution of economic activity and state income under the Israeli military governments between 1967 and 1993. The second period saw the evolution of economic activity and public revenues under the PA between 1994 and 2020. Fundamentally, this chapter establishes the prevalence and characteristics of the PA's dual rentierism. Chapter 4 examines the economic consequences of clearance revenue and foreign aid dependency. It investigates the effects of dual rentierism on the economic structure, tax collection, economic planning, and fiscal policy. The chapter details the PA's rentier trap by studying the PA's economic position in relation to the wider structure of the economy. Chapter 5 explores how dual rentierism shaped the formation of PA–society relations. It mobilises three influential representatives of Palestinian society to draw conclusions on how the PA's dual rentierism affected its ability to establish a social contract with its society. The chapter tracks the evolution of the PA's relationship with the NGO sector, the PA's own class of public servants and the Palestinian business community. Each representative was situated differently relative to the PA's rentier trap: the NGO sector directly competed for foreign aid disbursements with the PA, public servants were the main beneficiary of the PA's generous external income-funded salaries, and the business community held the key to maximising the PA's recovery rates of clearance revenue according to the clearance bill system. The chapter concludes with an investigation of the PA's success or failure in coercing or co-opting Palestinian society through its budget. Finally, the book concludes by reflecting on the broader theoretical contributions of the book for our understanding of states or political entities that are dependent on one or more source of external income while also identifying future areas of research.

## REFERENCES

Abbott, George C. 1970. 'Economic Aid as a Unilateral Transfer of Resources.' *Journal of Political Economy* 78, no. 6: 1213–27.

Ad-Duweik, Ammar. 2013. 'The Palestinian Political System under the Palestinian Authority.' In *Papers on the Palestinian Political System and Transition of Power*, 64–65. Ramallah: The Palestinian Institute for the Study of Democracy (Muwatin).

al-Madbouh, Ghada. 2017. 'The (Quasi-) Political System in Palestine.' In *Between State and Non-State: Politics and Society in Kurdistan-Iraq and Palestine*, edited by Gülistan Gürbey, Sabine Hofmann and Ferhad Ibrahim Seyder, 77–100. New York, NY: Palgrave Macmillan.

Beblawi, Hazem. 1987. 'The Rentier State in the Arab World.' In *The Rentier State: Nation, State and the Integration of the Arab World*, edited by Hazem Beblawi and Giacomo Luciani, Chapter 2. London: Croom Helm.

Berger, Mark T. 2006. 'From Nation-Building to State-Building: The Geopolitics of Development, the Nation-State System and the Changing Global Order.' *Third World Quarterly* 27, no. 1: 5–25.

Besley, Timothy and Torsten Persson. 2014. 'Why Do Developing Countries Tax So Little?' *Journal of Economic Perspectives* 28, no. 4: 99–120.

Bizhan, Nematullah. 2018. *Aid Paradoxes in Afghanistan: Building and Undermining the State*. London: Routledge.

Bräutigam, Deborah. 2008. 'Introduction.' In *Taxation and State-building in Developing Countries: Capacity and Consent*, edited by Deborah Bräutigam, Odd-Helge Fjeldstad, and Mick Moore. Cambridge: Cambridge University Press.

Brown, Nathan. 2003. *Palestinian Politics After the Oslo Accords: Resuming Arab Palestine*. Berkeley, CA: University of California Press.

Brynen, Rex. 1995. 'The Neopatrimonial Dimension of Palestinian Politics.' *Journal of Palestine Studies* 25, no. 1: 23–36.

Brynen, Rex. 2000. *A Very Political Economy*. Washington, DC: United States Institute of Peace Press.

Campbell, John L. 1993. 'The State and Fiscal Sociology.' *Annual Review of Sociology* 19: 163–85.

Ertman, Thomas. 1997. *Birth of the Leviathan: Building States and Regimes in Mediaeval and Early Modern Europe*. Cambridge: Cambridge University Press.

Fukuyama, Francis. 2007. 'Liberalism versus State-Building.' *Journal of Democracy* 18, no. 3: 10–13.

Goldscheid, Rudolf. 1958. 'A Sociological Approach to Problems of Public Finance.' In *Classics in the Theory of Public Finance*, edited by Richard Musgrave and Alan Peacock. London: Palgrave Macmillan.

Halper, Jeff. 2006. 'The 94 Percent Solution: Israel's Matrix of Control.' In *The Struggle for Sovereignty: Palestine and Israel 1993–2005*, edited by Joel Benin and Rebecca L. Stein, 62–70. Stanford, CA: Stanford University Press.

Hilal, Jamil. 2006. *The Palestinian Political System after Oslo: An Analytical Study*. Beirut: Palestine Studies Institute.

Iqtait, Anas. 2017. 'The Palestinian Authority and the Rentier State.' *Siyasat Arabiya* 26: 55–66.

Iqtait, Anas. 2021. 'The Palestinian Authority Political Economy: The Architecture of Fiscal Control.' In *Political Economy of Palestine*, 249–70. Cham: Palgrave Macmillan.

Jamal, Amaney A. 2007. *Barriers to Democracy: The Other Side of Social Capital in Palestine and the Arab World*. Princeton, NJ: Princeton University Press.

Jarbawi, Ali, and Wendy Pearlman. 2007. 'Struggle in a Post-Charisma Transition: Rethinking Palestinian Politics after Arafat.' *Journal of Palestine Studies* 36, no. 4: 6–21.

Jenkins, J. Craig, Katherine Meyer, Matthew Costello, and Hassan Aly. 2011. 'International Rentierism in the Middle East and North Africa, 1971–2008.' *International Area Studies Review* 14, no. 3: 3–31.

Kanafani, Nu'man. 2011. *As If There Is No Occupation: The Limits of Palestinian Authority Strategy*. Middle East Research and Information Project, September 22. https://merip.org/2011/09/as-if-there-is-no-occupation/.

Khalil, Assem. 2013. *Law of Legislation and Law of Liberty: Is Democracy an Alternative to the Rule of Law?* Ramallah: The Palestinian Institute for the Study of Democracy (Muwatin).

Levi, Margaret. 1999. 'Death and Taxes: Extractive Equality and the Development of Democratic Institutions.' In *Democracy's Values*, edited by Ian Shapiro and Casiano Hacker-Cordon, 112–31. Cambridge: Cambridge University Press.

Lia, Brynjar. 2006. *A Police Force without a State: A History of the Palestinian Security Forces in the West Bank and Gaza*. Reading: Ithaca Press.

Moore, Mick. 2001. 'Political Underdevelopment: What Causes "Bad Governance".' *Public Management Review* 3, no. 3: 358–418.

Moore, Mick. 2004. 'Revenues, State Formation, and the Quality of Governance in Developing Countries.' *International Political Science Review* 25, no. 3: 297–319.

Musgrave, Richard. 1992. 'Schumpeter's Crisis of the Tax State: An Essay in Fiscal Sociology.' *Journal of Evolutionary Economics* 2, no. 89: 89–113.

Rad, Sahar Taghdisi. 2015. 'Political Economy of Aid in Conflict: An Analysis of Pre- and Post-Intifada Donor Behaviour in the Occupied Palestinian Territories.' *International Journal of Security and Development* 4, no. 1: Art. 22.

Richter, Thomas and Christian Steiner. 2008. 'Politics, Economics and Tourism Development in Egypt: Insights Into the Sectoral Transformations of a Neo-patrimonial Rentier State.' *Third World Quarterly* 29, no. 5: 939–59.

Riddell, Roger C. 2008. *Does Foreign Aid Really Work?* Oxford: Oxford University Press.

Schumpeter, Joseph. 1991. The Crisis of the Tax State. *The Economics and Sociology of Capitalism*, edited by Richard Swedberg, 99–140. Princeton, NJ: Princeton University Press.

Tartir, Alaa, Sam Bahour, and Samer Abdelnour. 2013. 'Defeating Dependency, Creating a Resistance Economy.' *Al-Shabaka: The Palestinian Policy Network* (13 February 2013). https://al-shabaka.org/briefs/defeating-dependency-creating-resistance-economy/.

Telhami, Shibley. 2001. 'The Road to Palestinian Sovereignty: Problematic Structure or Conventional Obstacles?' In *Problematic Sovereignty: Contested Rules and Political Possibilities*, edited by Stephen Krasner, 301–22. New York, NY: Columbia University Press.

Weber, Max. 1978. *Economy and Society: An Outline of Interpretive Sociology.* Berkeley, CA: University of California Press.

World Bank. 1994. *Emergency Assistance Program for the Occupied Territories.* Washington, DC: World Bank.

World Bank. 2021. ODA Data Base. https://data.worldbank.org/indicator/DT.ODA.ODAT.PC.ZS.

CHAPTER 2

# Fiscal Sociology, Political Rents, and Dual Rentierism

**Abstract** This chapter offers a critical overview of how states' dependence on external income has been theorised. In particular, it looks at the classifications and effects of different types of rentier income and advances a theoretical framework for political rentierism. The chapter compares the characteristics of political rents and natural resource rents from the point of view of the accruing state and examines the effects of political rents on the economy, state–society relations, and taxation. In doing so, it has laid the foundations for the exploration of the effects of the two different sources of political rents on the PA.

**Keywords** Rentier State Theory · Dual rentierism · Political rents · Rentierism

In outlining the theoretical approach of the book, this chapter draws on literature from various disciplines, including political economy, international relations and international development. There are virtually no studies which analyse the Palestinian Authority's two main sources of revenue—foreign aid and clearance revenue—simultaneously and within the context of political economy. In particular, there are no studies that investigate how foreign aid and clearance revenue have influenced the Palestinian economy and shaped the decision-making process behind the

© The Author(s), under exclusive license to Springer Nature Switzerland AG 2023
A. Iqtait, *Funding and the Quest for Sovereignty in Palestine*,
https://doi.org/10.1007/978-3-031-19478-8_2

15

Palestinian Authority's economic policy and state–society relations. To address this gap, this chapter applies Rentier State Theory (RST) to dissect the political economy of the Palestinian Authority and proposes a modified rentier model to accommodate the specific characteristics of political rents and the Palestinian case. The chapter starts with a theoretical discussion on sources of state revenues and RST. The second section builds on RST to advance a theoretical framework for political rentierism by comparing the similarities and differences resulting from the state's reliance on natural resource rents or political rents. The chapter concludes with an overview of the current scholastic understanding of rentierism in Palestine.

## 2.1 Sources of State Revenues and RST

Sources of state revenue are fundamental in understanding states' patterns of policy-making and state–society relations. Schumpeter argues that states revenues are 'one of the best starting points for an investigation of society, especially … its political life' (1991). Levi notes that 'the history of state revenue production is the history of the evolution of the state' (1991, p. 1). She defines revenue as the 'income of the government' and argues that 'the greater the revenue of the state, the more possible it is to extend rule. Revenue enhances the ability of rulers to elaborate the institutions of the state, to bring more people within the domain of those institutions, and to increase the number and variety of the collective goods provided through the state' (1991, p. 2).

Studies of state revenue highlight that different sources of revenue have different implications for the evolution, development and behaviour of states (Timmons 2005; Snyder and Bhavnani 2005; Campbell 1993; Cheibub 1998). Mahdavy argued in 1970 that sources of state revenue induce diverse economic, political and institutional outcomes (Mahdavy 1997). Mahdavy's claim is supported by others who, like Levi, identify that contemporary states rely on two major sources of revenue: taxes and rents (M. Moore 2004; Beblawi 1987; Luciani 1987; Bräutigam et al. 2008; Levi 1988). Taxes are broadly defined as 'compulsory levies that are not necessarily related to particular benefits received' (Lotz and Morss 1967, p. 480). A state that derives the majority of its revenue from taxation is generally referred to as a 'tax state'. Rent, on the other hand, is defined by Beblawi as 'income derived from gift[s] of nature' such as natural resources, or unearned foreign income, such as remittances or foreign aid (Beblawi 1987, p. 49). Accordingly, a state that derives the majority of its revenue from rent income is defined as a 'rentier state' (Mahdavy 1997; Luciani 1987).

Schumpeter argues that the expansion of the 'tax apparatus' into the economy places constraints on governments and political representation. Unlike tax states, which must form a bargain with their societies and citizens in order to collect taxes, the absence, or weakness, of the tax apparatus in rentier states allows the state to remain autonomous from its citizens (Beblawi 1987). In other words, the state lacks a social contract with its society. In rentier states, the institutional and political structures that allow states to bargain with their societies and citizens are replaced by a 'rentier bargain', whereby states allocate material benefits in exchange for political quiescence (Beblawi 1987). Jenkins et al. (2011) define a rentier state as 'a government that is able to use its legitimate monopoly over territory to extract significant rents from international transactions and thereby become the dominant actor in the political economy'. Beblawi (1987) argues that the rentier state is a state in which rent situations dominate the economy; the state relies solely on externally generated rents; only a few citizens are engaged in rent creation (even though the majority may benefit from its allocation); and government is the principal recipient of rents. He stresses that there is 'no such thing as a pure rentier state', and rentier conditions and rentier income exist in all economies to different degrees (Beblawi 1987, pp. 51–52). A rentier state is an allocative, rather than extractive, state due to the absence of an effective tax base (Luciani 1987). Luciani (1987, p. 70) quantifies the predominance of rents in government revenues as at least 40 per cent for a state to qualify as a rentier state. He also emphasises the centrality of the state in the wider economy, by stressing that public expenditure of the rentier state represents a significant share of the gross domestic product (GDP) (Luciani 1987, p. 70).

Mahdavy, in the 1960s, was the first to introduce Rentier State Theory (RST) in an attempt to describe the impacts of rents on political and economic behaviour of Iran. He noted that resource wealth in Iran did not result in economic growth, as suggested by conventional development theories of resource-driven development (Auty 1993, 1997). Resource wealth alters the development path of the state, and creates dependence on income derived from the export of natural resources (Mahdavy 1997). For Mahdavy, not only is the rentier state dependent on rents, but its dependence on rents also leads to a structural distortion in the economy

18 A. IQTAIT

whereby the natural resource exports sector expands at the expense of more product-intensive sectors, such as manufacturing (Mahdavy 1997). RST provides an important framework for understanding the behaviour of many rent-dependent states, particularly in the Middle East. Anderson (1987, p. 9) applauds it as 'one of the major contributions of Middle East regional studies to political science'. On the other hand, Okruhlik (1999, p. 308) accuses RST of conceptual overstretch, noting that 'the idea of the rentier state has come to imply so much that it has lost its content'. Maloney (2008) argues that RST is incapable of explaining developments in the political economy environment in the Middle East. She claims that RST alone has little utility in addressing changing economic policies, state–society accountability and responsiveness paradigms, and foreign relations of the rentier states. Rosser (2006) suggests that RST has been addressed via a reductionist approach, wherein rents alone are blamed for the distortions observed in rentier states. He suggests instead addressing rentier states through a 'range of historical and other factors' at an individual country case level (Rosser 2006, p. 7).

RST theorists point to the importance of including pre-rent variables, incorporating international relations dynamics, and differentiating the role of different rent types. P. Moore highlights the importance of studying pre-rent socio-political realities in individual rentier states to understand the ramifications of rentierism (P. W. Moore 2004; see also Gray 2011). Such dynamics can include the prevalence of poverty and authoritarianism in the state prior to rent windfalls, as noted by Herb (2005). Additionally, Herb points to the role of the regional characteristics that could dictate rentierism, as most rentier states exist in regions with inherently low economic growth rates, suggesting that 'the natural resource trap may really be an African and Middle Eastern trap' (2005, p. 303). Other dynamics can include the uniqueness of the state formation paths of individual states. Schwarz (2008) observes that the context of historical experiences, socio-political conditions, existing institutionalism and business–government dynamics contributes to the mechanisms that link rentierism to the emergence of weak states. Rentier states often possess substantial deposits of mineral wealth or strategic importance, leading to considerable external influence and pressures that affect the evolution of different rentier states proportionally to the external variations. Luciani (1995; see also Sluglett 1995) highlights the significance of external major powers' influence on rentier Arab states in fuelling internal and regional instability and altering the behaviour and nature of the rentier state. As the structural premises of early RST were questioned and revised, a new understanding of rentierism emerged. RST evolved from a holistic political economy theory, allegedly capable of explaining the political and economic dynamics of the rentier states, to a framework with which to assess the characteristics of politics in rentier states. RST, therefore, represents the basic analytical frame for investigating the effects of external revenue streams to the central government on the country's economic and political character (Malik 2017). Although RST does not provide a comprehensive theory of the rentier state or predict the overall character of the rentier state, it points to a number of economic and political characteristics that typically emanate from a rentier economy.

These can be categorised into two groups. Firstly, rentierism hinders development by altering the economic structure of the state. Rentierism negatively affects economic diversification and economic growth, promotes short-term expenditure policies in lieu of sustainable development, and gives rise to a rentier mentality. Rentier states play a crucial role in domestic economic activity and represent a significant share of GDP due to inflated expenditure policies. Rentier states are fixated on short-term prosperity resulting from the mass allocation of rents (Malik 2017, p. 74). Luciani (1987, p. 74) echoes this premise and argues that the rentier state 'does not need to formulate anything deserving the appellation of economic policy: all it needs is an expenditure policy'. Although rentier states allocate massive sums of income to the economy, empirical evidence suggests poor economic growth performance. This is attributable to the over-accumulation of foreign capital from the sale of natural resources on the international market. Large flows of foreign capital lead to an exaggeration in the price of the local currency, which in turn reduces the international competitiveness of the manufacturing and other productive sectors in the local economy, lowers wages in these sectors, and sustains a vicious circle of dependence on rentier income. The negative consequences of dependence on rent are widely known as the 'resource curse' or 'the Dutch Disease' (Ross 1999; Bruno and Sachs 1982; Auty 1997; Davis and Tilton 2005).

The second group of characteristics, as suggested by M. Moore (2004), reflect that fact that rentierism results in 'political pathologies' that alter state–society relations. These include hindering the political evolution of the state to a representative form of governance, autonomy from citizens, authoritarianism, susceptibility to external intervention, non-transparency in public expenditure, and ineffective public bureaucracy (M. Moore 2004). Ross (2001) argues that there are three effects of rents that sustain non-democratic rule in rentier states. The first is the 'rentier effect', whereby the absence of wide taxation in society, large-scale spending on patronage, and forceful inhibition of the formation of societal groups keep society disengaged and buy political acquiescence for the state. The second effect is the 'repression effect', whereby rentier income leads to the creation of a repressive apparatus either for containing local dissent or for protecting resource wealth from regional or ethnic conflict. The third is borrowed from modernisation theory, according to which, in order for economic development to lead to democratisation, a combination of societal and cultural changes must occur, mainly at the educational level and occupational specialisation, whereas in rentier states socio-political stagnation persists, inhibiting democratisation (Ross 2001, pp. 332–36). Additional to Ross's arguments, Posusney (2004, p. 130) observes the inverse relationship between rentierism and political pluralisation, high-lighting the overwhelmingly 'single party states and party-less monarchies across the [Arab] region'. Yates (1996) goes further, arguing that, in a non-representative governance structure, state officials in rentier states can easily utilise rents to finance illegal or unpopular objectives, resulting in poor governance. Lam and Wantchekon (1999) further affirm the link between rentierism and authoritarianism, as economic growth and alloca-tion of political power in rentier states intertwine to favour higher income inequality and the strengthening of autocratic rule. This is also discussed by Karl (1997) in the context of the centralisation of power and resources arising from the co-optation of institutions.

Complementary to the preceding discussion, M. Moore (2004, p. 306) asserts that rentier states are autonomous from citizens because 'the state apparatus, and the people who control it, have a "guaranteed" source of income that makes them independent of their citizens'. Yergin (1991), M. Moore (2004), and Schwarz (2007) further claim that external inter-vention to protect strategic allies or natural resource wealth is a prominent feature of rentier states. M. Moore (2004, p. 306) also observes that 'this kind of relationship generally has increased the autonomy of oil states in relation to their citizens, most directly through external military and political support for regimes that enjoy little popular legitimacy'. External influence and autonomy from citizens fuel ineffective public bureaucracy and non-transparency in public expenditure. M. Moore adds: 'In the civil bureaucracy, jobs will be given mainly for patronage purposes and for directly political reasons' (M. Moore 2004, p. 308). This discussion certainly does not amount to a comprehensive model of the political and economic consequences of rents. It is merely a summary of what appear to be the key causal mechanisms that function in different circumstances. Although it may be tempting to embark on a detailed discussion examining the evolution of Rentier State Theory, to do so is beyond the scope of this book.

## 2.2   POLITICAL RENTS RENTIER STATES

Beblawi's early works on the rentier state stress that certain states 'receive consistent external income under political and strategic justifications' (Beblawi 1987, p. 60). He calls these states 'semi-rentiers' for their 'excessive reliance' on rents originating from development, budgetary and military aid, remittances, or location rents (Beblawi 1987, pp. 59–62). Luciani (1987) also asserts that RST, and certainly the rentier state phenomenon, is not necessarily limited to natural resource rentier states. M. Moore argues that there are two kinds of rentier states: the 'natural resource' rentier state and the 'political rent' rentier state. He defines political rent as 'surplus that can accrue to governments or to other organizations exercising effective territorial jurisdiction by virtue of either them as legitimate territorial authorities' (M. Moore 2004). While we have a wealth of literature that analyses the consequences of natural resource dependence, little attention has been allocated to the effects of non-natural resource external income dependency. This is particularly true with regards to states that rely on political rents in the form of foreign aid and other sources of fiscal revenues. The lack of literature in this field can be attributed to the fact that political rents are hard to quantify (M. Moore 2004, p. 305). The majority of this rent is foreign aid, and the modalities for its disbursement and allocation across different countries vary significantly. Political rents are also very diverse. They can accrue to the state in the form of development aid, budgetary support, military assistance, soft loans, and other forms of political rents, and can take the shape of financial assets or of material aid, such as food assistance or medical equipment. The vagueness of what constitutes political rents exacerbates the difficulty of quantifying the total value in a given period. Thus, the body of literature closest to understanding non-natural resource rentier states is generally limited to describing the consequences of foreign aid on the receiving state's economy, state-building, and state–society relations. In recent works, researchers such as Bizhan (2018), Verkoren and Kamphuis (2013), Lemay-Hébert and Murshed (2016), Iqtait (2017) and Isar (2014) have utilised RST to explore the impact of aid on state-building in several developing countries. Nonetheless, the overall literature on the utilisation of a political economic model to study the effects of political rents dependency remains sparse. As M. Moore (2004, p. 305) states: 'we do not have a general theory of the political economy of rentier states. In particular, our understanding of the political economy of states that depend on strategic rents remains relatively rudimentary and contestable'.

In defining political rents, it is important to comparatively analyse the characteristics of political rents and natural resource rents from the point of view of the accruing state. The first observation is that political rents and natural resource rents are both unearned and fungible sources of income for the state (M. Moore 2004). The concept of fungibility is best defined by White and Dijkstra (2003, p. 468) as 'the idea that aid pays not for the items which it is accounted for but for the marginal expenditure it makes possible'. Fungibility implies that the flow of rents replaces other forms of revenue for the state, thus increasing the dependence of the state on rentier income and eliminating other sources of potential revenue (White and Dijkstra 2003; Morrissey 2006; Leiderer 2012). For example, Smith (2008) and Morrison (2009) consider foreign aid as a highly fungible resource, acting similarly to oil in that it provides extra resources of income the government can use to distribute to its constituencies without taxation. Similarly, Feyzioglu et al. (1998) analyse the impact of foreign aid on the recipient country's budgetary allocation in order to determine its fungibility. In a sample that included 38 countries for a period of over 20 years and considered different components of political rents, such as concessionary loans and aid, they find that aid is fungible and is used to free up other resources for the state, with 'part of the funds … used for tax reduction' (Feyzioglu et al. 1998, p. 54). Griffin and Enos (1970) argue that political rents lead governments to increase domestic consumption and abstain from raising taxes. In line with this argument, M. Moore (2004) claims that political rents increase the financial autonomy of the state from its society by eliminating the need for taxation and diverting funds as it deems necessary. Djankov et al. (2008, p. 171) note that 'natural resources and foreign aid share a common characteristic: they can be appropriated by corrupt politicians without having to resort to unpopular, and normally less profitable, measures like taxation'. As such, the fungibility of political rents is evidenced in the freedom it provides the state in allocating public spending to different sectors, and in its releasing the state from relying on other methods for revenue generation, such as taxation. Both mechanisms accentuate the similarities between political rents and natural resource rents.

On the other hand, political rents do not share all the characteristics of natural resource rents. Notable differences include political rent's conditionality, consistency of flow, and the accountability paradigm tied to the process of securing state revenues. Aid conditionality is of paramount importance in understanding the political economy of political rent rentier states. Natural resource rents are derived from the sale of resources in the international market, and the rents accrued do not—at least in theory—come with any conditions on how and where to spend this revenue. With political rents, however, the issue of conditionality is contested. For example, Morrison (2010) argues that foreign aid shares the un-conditional characteristics of natural resource rents due to the absence of effective implementation of aid conditionality. His argument is supported by a wealth of research concluding that aid conditionality has little systematic impact on policy in developing nations (see, e.g., Heckelman and Knack 2008; Morrissey 2002; Ohler et al. 2012; Burnside and Dollar 2000). The failure of aid conditionality is attributed to local political forces in recipient countries that continually resist externally imposed conditions. Evidence shows that policies adopted because of conditionalities are often 'reversed or simply ignored in practice'. Additionally, Morrison concludes that donors have incentives that dictate the continuity of their aid disbursement beyond the effective implementation of their policy conditions (Morrison 2009, p. 61). Such incentives can be economic, political or strategic, mainly as tools for exerting influence. On the other hand, although less prevalent, recent works have provided a wide range of theoretical and empirical arguments in support of the effectiveness of aid conditionalities (Bearce and Tirone 2010). Theoretically, the strategic components that incentivised donors to marginalise the importance of their policy-oriented conditionality have largely disappeared in favour of an international agenda of structural policy reforms in aid-recipient countries (Dornan 2017). Consider the vibrant aid effectiveness debate embodied in the Paris Declaration on Aid Effectiveness of 2005 and the ensuing research on aid modalities and effective aid implementation. Empirically, recent research suggests correlation between reforms and foreign aid in the post-Cold War period, providing limited support to the conditionality of political rents argument (Dornan 2017; Bearce and Tirone 2010).

Natural resource rents present a more reliable source of revenue for the state than political rents. It is true that natural resource revenue is affected by price fluctuations in the international market, but the relative inelasticity in international demand for natural resources—mainly oil and natural gas—provides leverage in terms of income reliability. Political rents, on the other hand, are highly subject to the preferences of rent providers. Such preferences include the internal political objectives of donor countries or shifts in foreign policy orientations. Another aspect worth noting is the accountability of the state. As has been established, natural resource rentier states are autonomous from their citizens. Conversely, political rents tend to shift accountability in favour of the rent providers (Bräutigam 2002). This includes political and economic transparency vis-à-vis rent providers, in the form of public financial records management, economic data and political agreements (Bizhan 2018). Citizens do not have access to the same information. This shift in accountability in favour of rent providers may exacerbate some of the adverse effects of political rents on economy and state–society relations, as will be shown in the empirical section of this book in the case of the Palestinian Authority. The comparative examination between natural resource and political rents results in political rents being an equally fungible, more conditional and less consistent revenue source than natural resource rents. Political rents also alter the accountability of the state in favour of rent providers.

The above discussion points to the effects of political rents on the economy and state–society relations. This is best represented by the research on the 'aid curse', and the effects of unearned state income on governance and state formation. Foreign aid has been associated with an inverse correlation with economic growth and growth in labour-intensive industry and export sectors. Economic structural pathologies develop in aid-dependent economies similar to those that arise in natural resource rent-dependent economies. The argument is that large flows of foreign aid drive up the real exchange rate of the local currency, leading the manufacturing and production-oriented sectors in the economy to become less competitive abroad, and thereby redirecting labour and capital away from the non-rent dominant sectors, resulting in an overdependence on the flow of rents and exposure to fluctuations in the disbursements of said rents—a pathology also known as the 'Dutch Disease' (Rajana and Subramanian 2008, 2011; Prati and Tressel 2006; Montinola 2010). Djankov et al. (2008) conducted a study that quantified the effects of political and natural resource rents on democracy from over one hundred countries during a forty-year period, and concluded that political and natural resource rents exert similar effects on political institutions, governance, and democratic transition. Furthermore, they argue that external income results in the deterioration of existing political institutions. This deterioration accelerates the higher the rate of rents as percentage of GDP. Knack (2001) details evidence significantly linking foreign aid, both as a percentage of GDP or as percentage of government expenditure, to worsening performance of economic and political institutions and the quality of governance. He further investigated the results of political rents windfall on the overall quality of the tax system in developing countries, showing that foreign aid adversely affects the quality of the tax system in aid-dependent countries. Knack (2009) argues that dependence on aid provides fewer incentives to broaden the tax base, improve collection mechanisms and eliminate inefficient tax policies and corruption. These findings are echoed by Mahdavi (2008), Remmer (2004) and Bräutigam et al. (2008). Work by Collier (2006) and Auty (2006) also suggests that foreign aid can create dysfunctional rent-seeking behaviour that weakens the accountability of governments to their citizens.

However, recent research suggests that the relationship is more complex, and that foreign aid influences tax performance more erratically than natural resource rents. Crivelli et al. (2012) and Pivovarsky et al. (2003) agree with the general assumption that foreign aid reduces tax performance, but assert that the *composition* of aid plays an important role in determining the strength of this correlation. For example, budgetary grants discourage tax performance while concessional loans encourage tax collection. Teera and Hudson (2004) and Clist and Morrissey (2011) found mixed effects of foreign aid on the tax performance of recipient countries. Their main premise is that in order to fully capture the effects of aid on tax, the relationships between government spending, existing tax revenue flows and the flow of aid must be examined. Adopting this model reveals that the ratio of tax revenue to GDP varies the least with aid flows, suggesting that aid does not necessarily worsen the tax collection performance of the state. Finally, Prichard et al. (2012) highlight the role of existing tax institutions in recipient countries, and the importance of complementary donor policies to enhance tax performance with the flow of aid.

Taken together, the literature provides a mixture of evidence on the role of foreign aid on tax performance. However, there is agreement that states with weak institutions, and those that receive foreign aid in the form of grants rather than concessional loans, tend to be less consistent in their tax performance. These states also tend to be less transparent with their public expenditures. De Renzio and Angemi (2011) highlight an inverse relationship between budget transparency and aid-dependence. Ramkumar and de Renzio (2009) and Boyce and O'Donnell (2007) claim that donor countries press governments to improve their reporting on budgetary information to donors, but neglect to improve governments' transparency standards towards their societies and citizens. This process may distort local accountability, influence recipient governments' domestic policies, have a damaging impact on domestic legitimacy, and undermine the emergence of a domestic social contract (Boyce and O'Donnell 2007, pp. 10–12).

Political rents have thus been shown to produce varying economic and political effects. Economic impacts one can expect to observe include symptoms of the Dutch Disease, lack of economic diversification, and inconsistent or volatile rent-driven growth. The state's revenues are also expected to be primarily composed of rentier income, and its expenditure is expected to be expansive compared to domestic economic activity and GDP. Political impacts include the evolution of a rentier class and an inflated public sector, lack of democratic processes, authoritarian and repressive behaviour, deterioration in existing political institutions, and mistrust and competition between state and civil society. In addition, political rentier states are expected to show low levels of domestic tax collection, low transparency vis-à-vis citizens and weak domestic legitimacy.

## 2.3   Rents, Rentierism, and Palestine

Having put forward a theoretical framework of the political rents rentier state, this segment scans the existing literature pertaining to rents and rentierism in the Palestinian context. A critical distinction to highlight at this stage is the difference between rent-seeking behaviour in economics and rentierism within the political economy frameworks of RST (Khan 2004; Gray 1914). Khan (2004) conducted a thorough examination of the rent-seeking behaviour of the PA in its early years of formation, between 1994 and 2002. This research, however, did not provide an overview of rent-seeking behaviour by agents in the political economy; rather, it explored the impacts of rentierism on the Palestinian political economy vis-à-vis the economy and state–society relations. To this end, the review provided has laid the foundations of the theoretical approach of RST in political rentier states. The review that follows will deliver the current scholastic understanding of rentierism in Palestine.

Robinson noted in 1997 that the PA's reliance on donors and Israel for the bulk of its government revenues would likely create and sustain an authoritarian structure. He clarified that 'the Palestinian polity is fast becoming a rentier state, with all its attendant qualities: an authoritarian state unresponsive to social concerns; and a society compelled towards quiescence if it wishes to share in the distribution of scarce resources' (Robinson 1997). A decade later Neu et al. (2007, p. 20) confirmed Robinson's prediction, arguing that the PA's political economy had increasingly come to resemble those of the oil states in the Arab world, adding that the PA's rentier nature had prevented the formation of a social contract between state and society over the relationship between taxation and expenditures. They further argued that 'the one-way flow of resources from state to society tends to promote personalized authoritarianism' in Palestine (Neu et al. 2007, p. 20). Jensen (2005), Haddad (2013) and Parsons (2011) classified the PA as a rising semi-rentier government for its reliance on foreign aid.

In her study of the impact of what she called 'aid rentierism' on the responsiveness and political conduct of Palestinian political leadership, Schwarze (2016, p. 68) classified the Palestinian Authority as both a rentier state and, at times, a semi-rentier state due to the 'dependence of the PA on donor funds'. Schwarze argued that donors' policies hindered political engagement and association with the PLO after the creation of the PA in 1993. Donors' policies further undermined the PA's ability to establish local legitimacy. For Schwarze, foreign aid sustained networks of patronage and empowered a neopatrimonial system constructed around the PA's top leadership (Schwarze 2016). Dengler (2001) claimed that 'the attraction, appropriation and distribution of foreign funds became a major tool to establish a power base' in Palestine in lieu of establishing local representation. Moreover, aid distribution modalities within the PA, and its ability to function independently of the Palestinian public, created a system less concerned with representation and more drawn to individual power politics (Dengler 2001, p. 69). Foreign aid shifted the account-ability paradigm of the PA in favour of the donors at the expense of the local population. Ibrahim and Beaudet (2012) and Sayigh (2007) argue that, too often, the Palestinian leadership conformed to international demands rather than local popular aspirations and national objectives. The PA's aid rentierism resulted in widespread discriminatory practices of aid distribution, mismanagement of public funds and increasing public dissatisfaction with the PA's leadership (Ibrahim and Beaudet 2012; Sayigh 2007; Schwarze 2016; Iqtait 2021). Hovsepian (2008) addressed the effects of rentierism on the construction of Palestinian national identity via the educational curriculum, arguing that aid rentierism exacerbated existing deficiencies in the construction of a Palestinian national identity via independent educational curriculums. It influenced the PA's categorisation of priorities and strategies for the educational system, shedding light on the real 'limits of the power of the Palestinian state as it seeks to attain sovereignty' (Hovsepian 2008, p. 30).

In a related but different analytical approach, Roy (1995) suggested that the Palestinian economy of the West Bank and Gaza had undergone a process of de-development. De-development describes a structural relationship between a stronger (dominant) and weaker (subordinate) economy whereby the dominant economy systematically distorts and undermines the development process of the subordinate one. This structural relationship is based on expropriating and dispossessing the subordinate economy of key economic resources critical to the formation of essential productive capacity. It also involves integrating and externalising economic growth variables to be dependent on externally generated sources of income in the form of remittances and foreign aid. Finally, de-development relates to the process of deinstitutionalisation, whereby—in the case of Palestine—Israeli policies restricted the development of Palestinian institutions and undermined existing institutional structures. Roy (1995, p. 66) stated that

> [t]he de-development of an economy does not mean that individual production cannot be increased or individual living standards improved, as occurred in the West Bank and Gaza Strip during the first decade of Israeli occupation. Hence, although a process of structural change was clearly evident after 1967, it was aberrant change precluding the qualitative transformation of positive growth into sustained economic development.

The preceding discussion highlights the current understanding of rentierism in Palestine. The PA is classified as a rentier entity on occasion, but without a comprehensive framework for defining the nature and magnitude of its rentier income. The literature also supports the hypothesis that rentier income, particularly foreign aid is linked to the evolution and behaviour of the PA. However, the literature remains devoid of a RST approach to investigating the simultaneous effect of foreign aid and clearance revenue on the PA. In addition, there is a dearth of scholarship when it comes to studying the effects of rentier income on the Palestinian political economy.

## 2.4   Conclusion

The composition of state revenue influences states' policies, state–society relations and the wider economy. In particular, states that rely on rentier income for the majority of their revenue suffer from a broad set of political and economic pathologies. Consideration of pre-rent variables, international relations dynamics, and the role of different rent types is also critical in assessing the true impacts of rents. This chapter has distinguished between political rents and natural resource rents and suggested a modified RST framework to study the effects of political rentier income. In doing so, it has laid the foundations for the exploration of the effects of the two different sources of political rents on the PA.

The chapter developed a theoretical framework that will guide this research through three main themes. The first theme assumes the economic effects of rentier reliance to be composed of a number of economic distortions. These distortions include the presence of the Dutch Disease, weak economic diversification, and rent-driven and inconsistent or negative economic growth. The second theme involves fiscal distortions, which include the presence of economic policies characterised by an inflated public sector, high expenditure relative to GDP and an allocative policy whereby the majority of government expenditure is spent on wages and social transfers. Finally, rentier reliance can lead to a number of political effects that alter the state–society relationship. These effects include the creation of a rentier class, the prevalence of authoritarianism, the lack of political institutions, and continuous mistrust and competition between different segments of society and the state. These effects also hinder the evolution of a social contract based on taxation and representation, which in turn impedes democratic transition and creates weak domestic legitimacy.

Chapter 3 will establish the empirical basis of the rentier state in Palestine. It will identify the main sources of rents to the Palestinian economy and the PA from a historical perspective, and examine rentier income's prevalence by adopting concepts developed in this chapter. The subsequent chapters investigate the expected economic and political characteristics of the PA given its rentierism.

## REFERENCES

Anderson, Lisa. 1987. 'The State in the Middle East and North Africa.' *Comparative Politics* 20, no. 1: 9.

Auty, Richard M. 1993. *Sustaining Development in Mineral Economies: The Resource Curse Thesis.* London: Routledge.

Auty, Richard M. 1997. *Resource Abundance and Economic Development.* Oxford: Oxford University Press.

Auty, Richard M. 2006. *Aid and Rent-Driven Growth: Mauritania, Kenya and Mozambique Compared.* United Nations University (UNU)-WIDER Research Paper No. 2007/35.

Bearce, David, and Daniel Tirone. 2010. 'Foreign Aid Effectiveness and the Strategic Goals of Donor Governments.' *The Journal of Politics* 72, no. 3: 846.

Beblawi, Hazem. 1987. 'The Rentier State in the Arab World.' In *The Rentier State: Nation, State and the Integration of the Arab World*, edited by Hazem Beblawi and Giacomo Luciani, Chapter 2. London: Croom Helm.

Bizhan, Nematullah. 2018. *Aid Paradoxes in Afghanistan: Building and Undermining the State.* London: Routledge.

Boyce, James, and Madalene O'Donnell. 2007. 'Peace and the Public Purse: An Introduction.' In *Peace and the Public Purse: Economic Policies for Postwar Statebuilding*, edited by James Boyce and Madalene O'Donnell, 1–14. Boulder, CO: Lynne Rienner Publishers.

Bräutigam, Deborah. 2002. 'Building Leviathan: Revenue, State Capacity and Governance.' *IDS Bulletin* 33, no. 3: 10–18.

Bräutigam, Deborah, Odd-Helge Fjeldstad, and Mick Moore. 2008. *Taxation and State-building in Developing Countries: Capacity and Consent.* Cambridge: Cambridge University Press.

Bruno, Michael, and Jeffrey Sachs. 1982. 'Energy and Resource Allocation: A Dynamic Model of the Dutch Disease.' *The Review of Economic Studies* 49, no. 5: 845–59.

Burnside, Craig, and David Dollar. 2000. 'Aid, Policies, and Growth.' *The American Economic Review* 90, no. 4: 847–68.

Campbell, John L. 1993. 'The State and Fiscal Sociology.' *Annual Review of Sociology* 19: 163–85.

Cheibub, José Antonio. 1998. 'Political Regimes and the Extractive Capacity of Governments: Taxation in Democracies and Dictatorships.' *World Politics* 50, no. 3: 349–76.

Clist, Paul, and Oliver Morrissey. 2011. 'Aid and Tax Revenue: Signs of a Positive Effect Since the 1980s.' *Journal of International Development* 23, no. 2: 176–78.

Collier, Paul. 2006. 'Is Aid Oil? An Analysis of Whether Africa Can Absorb More Aid.' *World Development* 34, no. 9: 1482–97.

Crivelli, Ernesto, Sanjeev Gupta, Priscilla Muthoora, and Dora Benedek. 2012. *Foreign Aid and Revenue: Still a Crowding Out Effect?* IMF Working Paper No. 12/186.

Davis, Graham, and John Tilton. 2005. 'The Resource Curse.' *Natural Resources Forum* 29, no. 3: 233–42.

de Renzio, Paolo, and Diego Angemi. 2011. *Comrades or Culprits? Donor Engagement and Budget Transparency in Aid Dependent Countries*. IBEI Wording Paper 2011/33.

Dengler, Bettina. 2001. 'Sustainable Livelihoods and Farmers' Decision Making Behaviour in the West Bank.' Palestine, Conference on International Agricultural Research for Development. https://ftp.gwdg.de/pub/tropentag/proceedings/2001/full%20papers/13-migration/13_4_Dengler.pdf. Accessed 20 June 2017.

Djankov, Simeon, Jose Montalvo, and Marta Reynal-Querol. 2008. 'The Curse of Aid.' *Journal of Economic Growth* 13, no. 3: 171.

Dornan, Matthew. 2017 'How New Is the "New" Conditionality? Recipient Perspectives on Aid, Country Ownership and Policy Reform.' *Development Policy Review* 35, no. 1: 46–63.

Feyzioglu, Tarhan, Vinaya Swaroop, and Min Zhu. 1998 'A Panel Data Analysis of the Fungibility of Foreign Aid.' *World Bank Economic Review* 12, no. 1: 29–58.

Gray, Lewis Cecil. 1914. 'Rent under the Assumption of Exhaustibility.' *The Quarterly Journal of Economics* 28, no. 3: 466–89.

Gray, Matthew. 2011. *A Theory of 'Late Rentierism' in the Arab States of the Gulf*. Georgetown University School of Foreign Service in Qatar Occasional Paper No. 7.

Griffin, K. B., and J. L. Enos. 1970. 'Foreign Assistance: Objectives and Consequences.' *Economic Development and Cultural Change* 18, no. 3: 313–27.

32  A. IQTAIT

Haddad, Toufic. 2013 'Political Economy of Neoliberal Approaches to Conflict Resolution and Statebuilding in the Occupied Palestinian Territories 1993 to 2013.' *Bulletin for the Council for British Research in the Levant* 8, no. 1: 30–34.

Heckelman, Jac C., and Stephen Knack. 2008. 'Foreign Aid and Market-Liberalizing Reform.' *Economica* 75, no. 299: 524–48.

Herb, Michael. 2005. 'No Representation without Taxation? Rents, Development, and Democracy.' *Comparative Politics* 37, no. 3: 297–316.

Hovsepian, Nubar. 2008. *Palestinian State Formation: Education and the Construction of National Identity*. Newcastle: Cambridge Scholars Publishing.

Ibrahim, Nassar, and Pierre Beaudet. 2012. 'Effective Aid in the Occupied Palestinian Territories?' *Conflict, Security and Development* 12, no. 5: 481–500.

Iqtait, Anas. 2017. 'The Palestinian Authority and the Rentier State.' *Siyasat Arabiya* 26: 55–66.

Iqtait, Anas. 2021. 'The Palestinian Authority Political Economy: The Architecture of Fiscal Control.' In *Political Economy of Palestine*, 249–70. Cham: Palgrave Macmillan.

Isar, Sarajuddin. 2014. 'A Blessing or a Curse? Aid Rentierism and State-building in Afghanistan.' *E-International Relations* (May).

Jenkins, J. Craig, Katherine Meyer, Matthew Costello, and Hassan Aly. 2011. 'International Rentierism in the Middle East and North Africa, 1971–2008.' *International Area Studies Review* 14, no. 3: 6.

Jensen, Michael Irving. 2005. *Peace, Aid & Renewed Anti-Colonial Resistance: The Development of Secular Palestinian NGOs in the Post-Oslo Period*. Danish Institute for International Studies Working Paper No. 2005/7.

Karl, Terry Lynn. 1997. *The Paradox of Plenty: Oil Booms and Petro-States*. Berkeley, CA: University of California Press.

Khan, Mushtaq. 2004. 'Evaluating the Emerging Palestinian State: "Good Governance" Versus "Transformation Potential".' In *State Formation in Palestine*, in *State formation in Palestine: Viability and Governance during Social Transformation*, edited by Mushtaq Khan, George Giacaman, and Inge Amundsen, 13–63. London: Routledge.

Knack, Stephen. 2001. 'Aid Dependence and the Quality of Governance: A Cross-Country Empirical Test.' *Southern Economic Journal* 68, no. 2: 310–29.

Knack, Stephen. 2009. 'Sovereign Rents and Quality of Tax Policy and Administration.' *Journal of Comparative Economics* 37, no. 3: 359–71.

Lam, Ricky, and Leonard Wantchekon. 1999. *Political Dutch Disease*. New Haven, CT: Yale University Working Paper.

Leiderer, Stefan. 2012 *Fungibility and the Choice of Aid Modalities*. WIDER Working Paper No. 2012/68.

Lemay-Hébert, Nicolas, and Syed Mansoob Murshed. 2016. 'Rentier State-building in a Post-Conflict Economy: The Case of Kosovo.' *Development and Change* 47, no. 3: 517–41.

Levi, Margaret. 1988. *Of Rule and Revenue*. Berkeley, CA: University of California Press.

Lotz, Jørgen R., and Elliott R. Morss. 1967. 'Tax Effort in Developing Countries.' *International Monetary Fund* 14, no. 3: 480.

Luciani, Giacomo. 1987. 'Allocation Vs. Production States.' In *The Rentier State: Nation, State and the Integration of the Arab World*, edited by Hazem Beblawi and Giacomo Luciani, 64–80. London: Croom Helm.

Luciani, Giacomo. 1995. 'Oil and Political Economy in the International Relations of the Middle East.' In *International Relations of the Middle East*, edited by Louise Fawcett, 79–104. Oxford: Oxford University Press.

Mahdavi, Saeid. 2008. 'The Level and Composition of Tax Revenue in Developing Countries: Evidence from Unbalanced Panel Data.' *International Review of Economics and Finance* 17, no. 4: 607–17.

Mahdavy, Hussein. 1997. 'The Patterns and Problems of Economic Development in Rentier States: The Case of Iran.' In *Studies in Economic History of the Middle East*, edited by M.A. Cook, 428–67. Oxford: Oxford University Press.

Malik, Adeel. 2017. 'Rethinking the Rentier Curse.' In *Combining Economic and Political Development: The Experience of MENA*, edited by Giacomo Luciani, 41–57. Boston, MA: Brill-Nijhoff.

Maloney, Suzanne. 2008. 'The Gulf's Renewed Oil Wealth: Getting It Right This Time?' *Survival* 50, no. 6: 129–145.

Montinola, Gabriella R. 2010. 'When Does Aid Conditionality Work?' *Studies in Comparative International Development* 45, no. 3: 358–82.

Moore, Mick. 2004. 'Revenues, State Formation, and the Quality of Governance in Developing Countries.' *International Political Science Review* 25, no. 3: 197–319.

Moore, Pete W. 2004. *Late Development and Rents in the Arab World*. Paper presented at the annual meeting of the American Political Science Association, Hilton Chicago and the Palmer House Hilton, Chicago IL, September 2.

Morrison, Kevin. 2009. 'Oil, Nontax Revenue, and the Redistributional Foundations of Regime Stability.' *International Organization* 63, no. 1: 110.

Morrison, Kevin M. 2010. 'What Can We Learn about the "Resource Curse" from Foreign Aid?' *The World Bank Research Observer* 27, no. 1: 52–73.

Morrissey, Oliver. 2002. 'Conditionality and Aid Effectiveness Re-evaluated.' WIDER Project Meeting on Sustainability of External Development Financing in Helsinki (August).

Morrissey, Oliver. 2006. 'Fungibility, Prior Actions, and Eligibility for Budget Support.' In *Budget Support as More Effective Aid? Recent Experiences and*

34    A. IQTAIT

*Emerging Lessons*, edited by Stefan Koeberle, Zoran Stavreski and Jan Walliser, 333–43. Washington, DC: World Bank.

Neu, C. Richard, David Gompert, Glenn E. Robinson, Jerrold D. Green, and Kenneth Shine. 2007. *Building a Successful Palestinian State*. Arlington, VA: Rand Corporation.

Ohler, Hannes, Peter Nunnenkamp, and Axel Dreher. 2012. 'Does Conditionality Work? A Test for an Innovative US Aid Scheme.' *European Economic Review* 56: 138–53.

Okruhlik, Gwenn. 1999. 'Rentier Wealth, Unruly Law, and the Rise of Opposition.' *Comparative Politics* 31, no. 3: 308.

Parsons, Nigel. 2011. 'The Palestinian Authority Security Apparatus.' In *Surveillance and Control in Israel/Palestine: Population, Territory and Power*, edited by Elia Zureik, David Lyon, and Yasmeen Abu-Laban, 355–70. London: Routledge.

Pivovarsky, Alexander, Benedict Clements, Sanjeev Gupta, and Erwin Tiongson. 2003. *Foreign Aid and Revenue Response: Does the Composition of Aid Matter?* IMF Working Paper No. 3/176.

Posusney, Marsha Pripstein. 2004. 'Enduring Authoritarianism: Middle East Lessons for Comparative Theory.' *Comparative Politics* 36, no. 2: 130.

Prati, Alessandro, and Thierry Tressel. 2006. *Aid Volatility and Dutch Disease: Is There a Role for Macroeconomic Policies?* IMF Working Paper No. 06/145.

Prichard, Wilson, Jean-François Brun, and Oliver Morrissey. 2012. *Donors, Aid and Taxation in Developing Countries: An Overview*. International Centre for Tax and Development Working Paper 6.

Rajana, Raghuram, and Arvind Subramanian. 2008. 'Aid and Growth: What Does the Cross-Country Evidence Really Show?' *Review of Economics and Statistics* 90, no. 4: 643–65.

Rajana, Raghuram, and Arvind Subramanian. 2011. 'Aid, Dutch Disease, and Manufacturing Growth?' *Journal of Development Economics* 94, no. 1: 106–18.

Ramkumar, Vivek, and Paolo de Renzio. 2009. *Improving Budget Transparency and Accountability in Aid Dependent Countries: How Can Donors Help?* International Budget Partnership Brief No. 7 (IBP).

Remmer, Karen L. 2004. 'Does Foreign Aid Promote the Expansion of Government?' *American Journal of Political Science* 48, no. 1: 77–92.

Robinson, Glenn E. 1997. 'The Growing Authoritarianism of the Arafat Regime.' *Survival* 39, no. 2: 42–56.

Ross, Michael. 1999. 'The Political Economy of the Resource Curse.' *World Politics* 51, no. 2: 297–322.

Ross, Michael L. 2001. 'Does Oil Hinder Democracy?' *World Politics* 53: 332–37.

Rosser, Andrew. 2006. *The Political Economy of the Resource Curse: A Literature Survey*. Institute of Development Studies Working Paper 268. Brighton: University of Sussex.

Roy, Sara. 1995. *The Gaza Strip: The Political Economy of De-development*. Washington, DC: Institute of Palestine Studies.

Sayigh, Yezid. 2007. 'Inducing a Failed State in Palestine.' *Survival* 49, no. 3: 7–39.

Schumpeter, Joseph. 1991 'The Crisis of the Tax State.' In *The Economics and Sociology of Capitalism*, edited by Richard Swedberg, 99–140. Princeton, NJ: Princeton University Press.

Schwarz, Rolf. 2007. 'Rentier States and International Relations Theory.' Paper presented at the 6th Pan-European Conference on International Relations 'The Place of the Middle East in International Relations: Making Sense of Global Interconnection and Local Dynamics in Middle East Politics' (Turin, September).

Schwarz, Rolf. 2008. 'The Political Economy of State-Formation in the Arab Middle East: Rentier States, Economic Reform, and Democratization.' *Review of International Political Economy* 15, no. 4: 609.

Schwarze, Erika. 2016. *Public Opinion and Political Response in Palestine: Leadership, Campaigns and Elections since Arafat*. London: I.B. Tauris.

Sluglett, Peter. 1995. 'The Cold War in the Middle East.' In *International Relations of the Middle East*, edited by Louise Fawcett, 41–58. Oxford: Oxford University Press.

Smith, Alastair. 2008. 'The Perils of Unearned Income.' *The Journal of Politics* 70, no. 3: 780.

Snyder, Richard, and Ravi Bhavnani. 2005. 'Blood, and Taxes: A Revenue-Centered Framework for Explaining Political Order.' *The Journal of Conflict Resolution* 49, no. 4: 563–97.

Teera, Joweria, and John Hudson. 2004. 'Tax Performance: A Comparative Study.' *Journal of International Development* 16, no. 6: 794–95.

Timmons, Jeffrey F. 2005. 'The Fiscal Contract: States, Taxes, and Public Services.' *World Politics* 57, no. 4: 530–67.

Verkoren, Willemijn, and Bertine Kamphuis. 2013. 'State Building in a Rentier State: How Development Policies Fail to Promote Democracy in Afghanistan.' *Development and Change* 44, no. 3: 501–26.

White, Howard, and Geske Dijkstra. 2003. *Program Aid and Development: Beyond Conditionality*. London: Routledge.

Yates, Douglas. 1996. *The Rentier State in Africa: Oil Rent Dependency and Neo-colonialism in the Republic of Gabon*. Trenton, NJ: Africa World Press.

Yergin, Daniel. 1991. *The Prize: The Epic Quest for Oil, Money and Power*. New York, NY: Simon and Schuster.

CHAPTER 3

# Fiscal and Economic History of the West Bank and Gaza Strip

**Abstract** This chapter describes the presence and prevalence of external income in the Palestinian economy in a historical context. It delineates the Palestinian economy's dependence on external income over two distinct periods—the evolution of economic activity and public revenues under the Israeli military governments between 1967 and 1993, and the prevalence of external income and the fiscal composition of the Palestinian Authority since 1994. This historical approach is used to assess whether the Palestinian economy was inherently dependent on external income prior to the PA's establishment. The chapter concludes that economic activity and public revenues in the West Bank and Gaza have historically been shaped by Israel's political and economic policies and disproportionately relied on external income. It demonstrates that the fiscal character of the West Bank and Gaza has predominantly been defined by external income since 1967. It points to the increase in this reliance since the creation of the PA with its public revenues composed of 76 per cent of foreign aid and the Israeli-controlled clearance revenue. In addition, the Palestinian economy is found to be rent-driven, with a rent-to-GDP ratio of 37 per cent.

**Keywords** Clearance revenue · Foreign aid · Remittances · Public revenues · Allocative expenditure policy

© The Author(s), under exclusive license to Springer Nature Switzerland AG 2023
A. Iqtait, *Funding and the Quest for Sovereignty in Palestine*,
https://doi.org/10.1007/978-3-031-19478-8_3

## 3.1 Introduction

The economy that the Palestinian Authority (PA) inherited in the West Bank and Gaza in 1994 relied significantly on external income in the form of remittances and foreign aid. Successive Israeli military governments between 1967 and 1994 obstructed the evolution of a viable private sector, restricted capital flows, and spent inadequate sums on public investment. Instead, they sought to increase Palestinian income without developing the local economy by absorbing Palestinian labour in Israeli markets and transferring their income to the West Bank and Gaza in the form of remittances. When the PA was established, the World Bank and other international institutions speculated that injecting large sums of foreign aid would spur sustainable economic development and reduce Palestinian's reliance on external income. This approach, of funnelling large sums of foreign aid, has had major implications for the PA and the wider Palestinian economy. Although Palestinian GDP grew by around 600 per cent between 1994 and 2020, Palestinian reliance on external income has not reduced.

Despite this, research on the Palestinian economy has not hitherto investigated the prevalence and composition of external income available to the Palestinian economy and the PA. This chapter aims to fill this gap in order to empirically establish whether the Palestinian economy and the PA are dependent on rents. This is accomplished by determining Palestinian economic reliance on external income since 1967. This historical approach is adopted in order to identify whether the Palestinian economy was inherently dependent on external income prior to the PA's establishment in 1993. The chapter then outlines the evolution of the fiscal composition of successive governments in the West Bank and Gaza between 1967 and 2020. This includes the Israeli military governments between 1967 and 1993, and the PA since 1994.

The chapter establishes the empirical basis for describing the Palestinian economy as a rentier economy and the PA as a rentier entity. This will be theoretically guided by the modified rentier framework developed in Chapter 2. Beblawi and others have argued for classifying remittances and foreign aid as rentier income to the wider economy (Richter and Steiner 2008; Jenkins et al. 2011; Moore 2004; Beblawi 1987). Moreover, in the case of the PA, foreign aid and clearance revenue are externally accrued and controlled forms of revenue and will be classified as rentier income. The chapter will examine the prevalence of these sources of rentier income relative to Palestinian GDP and overall PA revenue. This will be accomplished by compiling data obtained from PA sources, such as statistical databases and publications by the Palestinian Central Bureau of Statistics (PCBS), Ministry of National Economy, and Ministry of Finance and Planning; international organisations and donors sources, such as World Bank, International Monetary Fund (IMF), United States Agency for International Development (USAID) and European Union databases, press releases, reports and publications; and Israeli sources, such as the Israeli Central Bureau of Statistics (ICBS) periodic reports and publications between 1967 and 1994. The chapter is partitioned into two sections. It begins with a description of the economic structure of the West Bank and Gaza under the Israeli military governments. It also investigates the main sources of public revenues which accrued to the Israeli military governments between 1967 and 1993. The outline is then extended to the PA era since 1994, with a sub-section on the sources and prevalence of rentier income. The final section describes the evolution of public revenues and expenditures by studying the PA's budget and fiscal policy since 1994.

## 3.2 Structural Basis for Rentierism: The Palestinian Economy, 1967–1993

Khouri (1980) argues that Israel's occupation of the West Bank and Gaza transformed it into a state with an imperial economy, relying on the captive economic resources and markets of occupied territories. He maintains that 'unlike the global empires of the last two centuries, where mother states relied on economic resources sent back by colonial outposts thousands of kilometres away, the Israeli imperial economy is based on resources located in geographically contiguous areas, making the process of political pacification, and subsequent economic domination, easier, more efficient and less obvious' (Khouri 1980, p. 71). The Israeli economic and fiscal policies in the West Bank and Gaza between 1967 and 1993 were typically unilaterally imposed by the Israeli government to serve Israeli political, military and economic interests as perceived at the time (Gazit 1995; World Bank 1993; Diwan and Shaban 1999). The Israeli government ran a fiscally conservative policy; often the revenues accruing to Israel from the West Bank and Gaza exceeded expenditures, thus resulting in a net gain to the Israeli treasury (Roy 1995, pp. 192–98). The administration spent very little on infrastructure, health, education,

40 A. IQTAIT

or public services. Israel's currency—first the lira, then the shekel—served as the predominant medium of exchange for the majority of daily economic transactions in the West Bank and Gaza (Arnon and Spivak 1996). This has continued to the present day, with the PA operating its budget in Israeli shekel. The utilisation of the shekel further reflected the absence of a central bank or Palestinian monetary policy. In addition, the Palestinian economy served as an extension of the larger and more developed Israeli economy. Samara argues that this structure was designed to coerce the Palestinian economic productive base to serve Israeli economic development needs, and to restrict the Palestinian economy's ability to trade with neighbouring states (Samara 2000).

In the early 1990s, it became clear that the Israeli economic and fiscal policies in the West Bank and Gaza had systematically stripped the local economy of its ability to develop. In 1991, the Israeli defence minister, Moshe Arens, appointed a committee to examine the means to develop the economy of the Gaza Strip, which produced one of the most elucidating statements regarding Israel's policy towards the Palestinian economy:

> In promoting the economic interests of the [Palestinian] population, the focus was on wage earners and on the short run. Regarding wage earners, priority was given to increasing their income by employing them in the Israeli economy. Only rarely did the policy opt for the development of an infrastructure and the encouragement of the creation of factories and employment within the Gaza Strip itself. No priority was given to the promotion of local entrepreneurship and the business sector in the Gaza Strip. Moreover, the authorities discouraged such initiatives whenever they threatened to compete in the Israeli market with existing Israeli firms. (Report of the Sadan Committee on the Gaza Area, as quoted in Arnon and Weinblatt 2001, p. 295)

The Sadan Committee's report identified Israel's role in evolving an economy that was predominantly reliant on external income. Remittances from wage earners employed in Israel, or elsewhere, financed the bulk of activity in the Palestinian economy between 1967 and 1993. This specific Israeli policy—of increasing income levels through employment in Israeli markets—resulted in intertwining Palestinian labour with the availability of external income in the Palestinian economy. The Palestinian labour market in 1993 had three characteristics. The first was related to demographics: a burgeoning youth population and a rapid decline in outward migration. The percentage of the population under the age of 14 had increased from 45 per cent in 1980 to more than 51 per cent in 1993. At the same time, emigration dropped from an annual average of more than 5 per cent in the early years of Israel's control over the West Bank and Gaza to less than 0.5 per cent in 1993 (ICBS 1996). This came as a result of tightening measures for Palestinian immigration to Arab Gulf states and Jordan.

The second characteristic concerned the non-productive composition and sectoral makeup of the economy. The non-productive services and construction sectors were disproportionately large, forming at least 65 per cent of the economy. The industrial sector, however, formed only seven per cent of the economy (ICBS 1996). This distortion was accompanied by a long-standing structural mismatch between education and market needs, which exacerbated the erosion of industrial or productive sectors (Newman 1984). The third characteristic of the labour market between 1968 and 1993 was a volatile macroeconomic environment. The West Bank and Gaza suffered from extreme economic expansion and contraction cycles. For example, GDP grew by more than 23 per cent in 1972, receded by eight per cent in 1973, and expanded again by 31 per cent in 1974. Similarly, it grew by 26 per cent in 1990 only to contract by seven per cent in 1991 (ICBS 1996). Growth and contraction cycles were extreme, affecting the stability of the larger labour market and hindering the ability of businesses to expand or provide long-term job security.

These three characteristics reflected the structural ineffectiveness of local labour markets in expanding employment. Within this context, Israeli officials and academics long understood the economic benefits of granting access to Palestinian employment in Israeli markets. The benefits stemmed from the abundant supply of cheap labour while transferring the social costs typically associated with foreign labour to the West Bank and Gaza. As a result, Palestinian employment in Israel accounted for 40 per cent of overall Palestinian employment by the end of the 1980s. As Fig. 3.1 illustrates, nearly 12 per cent of the total Palestinian labour force was employed in Israel in 1970; by 1990, this had jumped to 36 per cent (ICBS 1996). As much as 46 per cent of the Gaza Strip's labour force was employed in Israel in the mid-1980s (ICBS 1996). As such, Palestinian employment in Israel constituted an essential feature of the economic structure prior to 1993. This employment resulted in linking labour activity with the availability of external income to the wider economy and evolved as a direct result of Israel's economic policies.

For Israeli officials, utilising Palestinian labour was essential to improving living conditions and increasing income levels in the occupied territories without committing Israel to direct economic development of the areas.

External income from remittances and foreign aid represented a vital element of the Palestinian economy between 1967 and 1993. Remittances from Palestinian labour in Israel represented the bulk of external income to the Palestinian economy between 1967 and 1993. ICBS estimates that nearly two-thirds of Palestinian remittances during this period originated from labourers' wages in Israel, and constituted on average at least 18 per cent of the Palestinian gross national product (GNP) (ICBS 1996). The remainder of the remittances were from Palestinian labour in Jordan or other Arab countries (Mansour 1988, pp. 81–82). Foreign aid, being the second major source of external income, financed a portion of GNP, but the lack of disaggregated available data on aid transfers from 1967 to 1993 makes the assessment of aid contributions difficult. It is true that ICBS's National Accounts data reveal that although remittances represented the majority of external income to the West Bank and Gaza during that period, they alone cannot account for the presence of external income in the Palestinian economy. This is shown by examining the use of local resources in the West Bank and Gaza relative to GNP, which in this case suggests a wide gap between local production and overall consumption.

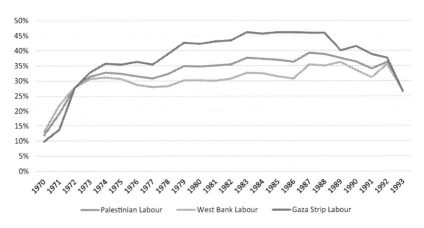

Fig. 3.1 Percentage of Palestinian labour force employed in Israel, 1970–1993 (Calculated from ICBS [1996] data)

This deficit, between local consumption and local production, is bridged via external income that cannot entirely be explained by remittances.

Therefore, there is empirical evidence for the presence of foreign aid in the West Bank and Gaza prior to 1994, with studies offering varying accounts of its quantity and effects. Mansour explains that foreign aid during this period was provided by five major donors: the Joint Jordanian-Palestinian Committee to Support the Steadfastness of the Palestinian People in the Occupied Homeland, the PLO, the Jordanian Government, USAID, the European Economic Community (EEC) and the United Nations (Mansour 1988, pp. 81–82). The Jordanian-Palestinian Committee was the most important source of foreign aid. The Committee started operating in 1979 and invested heavily in social services, construction and infrastructure projects, but investments in productive sectors were insignificant. Between 1979 and 1985, only 12.5 per cent of funds were disbursed to productive sectors such as industry and agriculture. It is estimated that the Committee had an annual budget of USD 100 million in 1982 (General Secretariat of the Joint Committee 1987). There are, however, no cumulative data on funds transferred by the PLO and the Jordanian government, but aid from these sources routinely financed budgets of municipalities, universities and charitable societies in the West Bank and Gaza between 1967 and 1993 (Nakhleh 1989). The United States Congress initiated a programme of economic assistance to the West Bank and Gaza in 1975. The purpose of the programme was to 'support projects and expand institutions in the occupied territories of the West Bank and Gaza to help build the socioeconomic underpinnings necessary to preserve peace' (Committee on Foreign Affairs 1979). The programme was administered by USAID through grants to private voluntary organisations operating in the West Bank and Gaza. Projects had to be approved by USAID and the Israeli military, which often diverted funds from the product manufacturing and industry sectors towards projects related to infrastructure and public works (Roy 1991). Between 1975 and 1991, about USD 100 million was approved and allocated to hundreds of projects (Roy 1991, p. 65). In a similar vein, the European Economic Community funded several European NGOs operating primarily in the vocational training and agricultural sectors. The EEC had an annual budget of more than USD 1 million in 1981 (Mansour 1988, p. 83). The United Nations was also a major source of foreign aid in the West Bank and Gaza. In addition to the United Nations Relief and Works Agency, the United Nations Development Program (UNDP) delivered a number

44    A. IQTAIT

of projects in the fields of education, health and agriculture. More than USD 12 million was disbursed between 1982 and 1986 (Mansour 1988, p. 84).

### 3.2.1  *Israeli Military Governments' Budget, 1967–1993*

The Israeli military governments maintained a strong record of fiscal extraction in the West Bank and Gaza. Public services provision was divided into three distinct sub-sectors: central bureaucracy represented by the Israeli military governments of the West Bank and Gaza between 1967 and 1993 (including the civil administration from 1981 to 1993); local government units represented by the semi-independent municipal and village councils; and NGOs and other international organisations (Gazit 1995). Fiscal extraction and processing was a function exclusive to the central bureaucracy with the assistance of local government units. The Israeli military governments undertook the responsibility of providing basic public services such as education, health, the judicial system and other central bureaucratic services to the Palestinians in the West Bank and Gaza (Bregman 2014). Fiscal revenues raised by Israel's military governments to finance expenditures originated from several sources. The first was taxes extracted from firms and individuals, such as income and property taxes. The second was revenue accruing to the Israeli government from Palestinian labourers in Israel. This revenue is derived from three sources: income taxes, national insurance fees, and pension contributions deducted from Palestinian labourers' pay (Hiltermann 1991). The third source was custom clearance revenue, which was largely associated with imports into the West Bank and Gaza. Last, and least important, were monetary transfers by international organisations, foreign countries or, rarely, the Israeli government (Arnon et al. 1997b, pp. 127–28).

The majority of these sources can be divided into three categories as shown in Table 3.1: direct taxation, indirect taxation and external transfers. Indirect taxation and external transfers represented most revenue accrued and averaged 54 per cent of total revenue between 1968 and 1993. Indirect taxes were the main source of revenue at the beginning of the period but declined in importance after 1973. This may be explained by the sharp increase in the number of Palestinian labourers working in Israel and paying high rates of income tax. Higher employment in Israel translated to an increase in the share of direct taxes from overall revenues. In 1968–1975 direct taxes averaged less than 30 per cent of total revenue

3 FISCAL AND ECONOMIC HISTORY OF THE WEST BANK ...    45

but rose to more than 52 per cent in 1974–1993. The share of indirect taxes dropped from 85 per cent in 1968 to less than 50 per cent in 1993. Table 3.1 also juxtaposes revenue and public expenditure. The Israeli military government divided expenditures into two categories: public investment and public consumption. Public investment typically

**Table 3.1** Public expenditures and revenues in the West Bank and Gaza, 1968–1993 (million New Israeli Shekel [ILS], 1986 prices)

| Year | Expenditures | | | Revenues | | | |
|---|---|---|---|---|---|---|---|
| | Public investment | Public consumption | Total expenditures | Direct taxes | Indirect taxes | Transfers and other | Total revenues |
| 1968 | 21.4 | 121.7 | 143.1 | 6.9 | 30.7 | 8.8 | 46.4 |
| 1969 | 40.4 | 138.3 | 178.7 | 15.9 | 32.8 | 6.7 | 55.4 |
| 1970 | 38.0 | 161.0 | 199.0 | 23.3 | 41.9 | 6.3 | 71.5 |
| 1971 | 38.5 | 168.7 | 207.2 | 28.2 | 45.1 | 5.2 | 78.5 |
| 1972 | 47.8 | 179.2 | 227.0 | 38.0 | 49.8 | 7.8 | 95.6 |
| 1973 | 48.4 | 182.5 | 230.9 | 61.8 | 48.5 | 17.3 | 127.6 |
| 1974 | 57.2 | 185.9 | 243.1 | 61.8 | 60.6 | 22.3 | 144.7 |
| 1975 | 75.3 | 182.7 | 258.0 | 77.5 | 49.4 | 29.4 | 156.3 |
| 1976 | 54.0 | 187.3 | 241.3 | 79.6 | 47.2 | 26.4 | 153.2 |
| 1977 | 41.5 | 188.3 | 229.8 | 76.9 | 53.4 | 20.3 | 150.6 |
| 1978 | 55.5 | 192.2 | 247.7 | 88.8 | 50.1 | 20.3 | 159.2 |
| 1979 | 52.5 | 197.6 | 250.1 | 102.2 | 39.3 | 20.8 | 162.3 |
| 1980 | 43.0 | 193.7 | 236.7 | 103.3 | 49.3 | 20.9 | 173.5 |
| 1981 | 48.9 | 196.2 | 245.1 | 115.7 | 63.9 | 23.7 | 203.3 |
| 1982 | 62.3 | 196.1 | 258.4 | 115.8 | 81.2 | 19.8 | 216.8 |
| 1983 | 75.8 | 201.3 | 277.1 | 138.5 | 257.9 | 16.1 | 412.5 |
| 1984 | 82.9 | 207.7 | 290.6 | 160.4 | 158.1 | 16.0 | 334.5 |
| 1985 | 73.6 | 208.5 | 282.1 | 126.0 | 123.0 | 14.3 | 263.3 |
| 1986 | 92.4 | 233.1 | 325.5 | 114.8 | 102.0 | 14.3 | 231.1 |
| 1987 | 121.9 | 252.3 | 374.2 | 126.9 | 92.0 | 31.7 | 250.6 |
| 1988 | 67.0 | 223.0 | 290.0 | 113.0 | 63.5 | 13.5 | 190.0 |
| 1989 | 54.0 | 238.0 | 292.0 | 137.0 | 64.9 | 16.3 | 218.2 |
| 1990 | 57.0 | 303.0 | 360.0 | 132.7 | 91.7 | 22.4 | 246.8 |
| 1991 | 83.0 | 295.0 | 378.0 | 172.0 | 128.9 | 21.3 | 322.2 |
| 1992 | 94.2 | 357.0 | 451.2 | 185.6 | 161.2 | 24.7 | 371.5 |
| 1993 | 162.1 | 365.0 | 527.1 | 166.3 | 142.0 | 27.7 | 336.0 |

*Source* ICBS, Arnon et al. (1997b, pp. 122–32)

46    A. IQTAIT

included expenditure on infrastructure, schools, roads, telecommunications, sewage, and health services. Compared to regional and international standards, public investment levels in the West Bank and Gaza under Israel's control were extremely low (Arnon et al. 1997b, p. 124; World Bank 1993), averaging just 3.4 per cent of GDP in the West Bank and 5.7 per cent in Gaza between 1968 and 1993 (ICBS 1996). Public investment levels also averaged less than 20 per cent of total Israeli expenditures in the territories. The remaining 80 per cent represented public sector expenditures on goods and services, which included spending by the central authority and municipalities. Finally, the public consumption share of GDP represented a mere 11 per cent in the West Bank and 14 per cent in Gaza between 1968 and 1993 (ICBS 1996). Table 3.1 indicates the presence of a continued public sector deficit from 1968 to 1993, but provides little insight regarding the funds used to offset this deficit. The consistent appearance of the annual deficit in Israeli data is further exacerbated by the lack of accumulation of local or international debt to finance the deficit. Arnon et al. (1997c), Benvenisti (1987) and Gharaibeh (1985) maintain that this gap can be explained by two factors—under-reporting of external transfers in the form of foreign aid, and misreporting of indirect taxation by excluding VAT and customs duties on imports destined for the West Bank and Gaza from or through Israel. When these forms of indirect taxes are added to the data, a consistent public sector *surplus* appears to be the norm (Arnon et al. 1997a; Hamed and Shaban 1994). This implies a much larger share of external transfers and indirect taxes as percentage of total revenues between 1968 and 1993, which is a structure that resembles the PA's revenues after 1994.

The high percentage of indirect taxes and external transfer of total revenue did not, however, prevent Palestinians from experiencing excessive taxation on income. Baxendale conducted a comparative examination on the taxation of income in Israel and the West Bank in 1989 and demonstrated that West Bank wage earners paid significantly more tax as a percentage of income than similarly positioned Israeli wage earners. This higher tax liability resulted from the Israeli military government's decision to decrease the intervals between tax rates for Palestinian wage earners (Baxendale 1989, pp. 139–40). This issue gained prominence in Palestinian–Israeli politics in 1989, when Palestinians across the West Bank refused to pay taxes to the Israeli authorities (Cowell 1989). In addition, the PLO managed to politicise the issue and urged Palestinians to stop paying taxes to the Israeli government in 1989, after the eruption of the Palestinian Intifada in 1987 (Author interview with Ishaq Jad, Bethelehem 2017). The Intifada's Unified Command's 'Call No. 6' urged Palestinians to boycott Israel economically, including by 'not paying taxes' (as quoted in Cobban 1990, p. 222).

The preceding overview of sources of external income in the economy and the fiscal structure of governments raises two points. The first is that the share of total external income in the form of remittances and foreign aid from the local economy in the West Bank and Gaza was significant, averaging 29 per cent of GNP between 1968 and 1993 (ICBS 1996). This dependence on external income was a result of Israeli economic and political policies. An asymmetrical relationship rose between Palestinian and Israeli markets, whereby Palestinian labour contributed to economic productivity in Israeli markets and, in exchange, the Palestinian economy received much-needed income. This policy of substituting Palestinian economic development with external income conditioned the health of the economy on the continuous and uninterrupted flow of this external income. Although less prevalent than remittances, Israeli policies also steered foreign aid away from productive projects into infrastructural and public works (Mansour 1988, p. 84). The second important point to consider is that most fiscal revenue generated in the West Bank and Gaza originated from economic activity in, with or through the Israeli economy. For example, income taxes collected at the time mostly accrued from Palestinian labourers working in Israeli markets. In addition, most indirect taxes, VAT and customs duties on imports accrued as a result of trade between the Palestinian and Israeli markets, or from imports that arrived through Israeli points of entry. This entailed that when the Palestinian Authority was established in the West Bank and Gaza after 1994, most of the existing tax base was controlled by Israel.

## 3.3 Palestinian Rentierism: Sources and Prevalence of External Income in Palestinian Economy, 1994–2020

The Palestinian Authority inherited an economic structure enervated by decades of marginalisation, dependence on Israel's economy, high unemployment and reliance on external income. Thus, when the Oslo process began Palestinian economic priorities were enhancing private sector growth, employment generation, ending dependency on Israel and lessening the reliance on external income (Roy 1999). The Palestinians needed to undertake large investments in infrastructure to offset decades of under-investment in electricity, communication, health, education and transportation. In essence, the PA was tasked with the process of developing a largely under-developed economy (Roy 1998). However, the structural relationship between the Palestinian and Israeli economies, and the excessive reliance on remittances and foreign aid, did not change after Oslo. In fact, economic and fiscal indicators prove that dependence on external income accelerated and became entrenched after the creation of the PA.

Between 1995 and 2020, remittance flows and prevalence relative to GDP increased significantly, making Palestine one of the largest recipients of remittances in the world. Remittances as a proportion of GDP in 2020 were around 17 per cent, placing Palestine in the top ten recipients of remittances (World Bank, n.d.(a)). Moreover, the proportion of remittances to GDP averaged around 15 per cent between 1995 and 2020 (World Bank, n.d.(b)). About 60 per cent of all remittances were in the form of workers' compensation transfers and nearly 90 per cent of all compensation transfers accrued from Palestinian labour in Israel (PCBS, n.d.). Figure 3.2 showcases the evolution of remittances transfers since 1994 and displays their value in US dollars and relative to GDP.

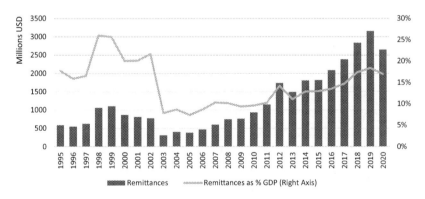

**Fig. 3.2** Remittances flow to Palestinian economy (current USD and relative to GDP), 1995–2020 (Calculated from data by World Bank [n.d.(b)])

Palestinian employment in Israel remained a significant source of external income for the Palestinian economy. Figure 3.3 highlights the absorption of the Palestinian labour force into Israeli labour markets and disaggregates employment figures between the West Bank and Gaza. While around 40 per cent of the Palestinian labour force was employed in Israeli markets in the 1980s, the average rate of employment did not exceed 13 per cent after 1994. Israel introduced policies in the early 1990s that severely restricted the flow of Palestinian labour and goods into Israel, and even within the West Bank and Gaza (United Nations Office for the Coordination of Humanitarian Affairs [OCHA] 2019). The United Nations estimates that there were 705 closure obstacles, in the form of checkpoints, roadblocks and other physical obstacles, that restricted Palestinian movement and access in the West Bank and Gaza (OCHA 2019). The introduction of these obstacles in the 1990s resulted in a structural change in the links between the Palestinian and Israeli economies, which led to a severe economic crisis and a decline in volume of Palestinian labour in Israel and, thus, the availability of this external income (Arnon and Weinblatt 2001).

Against this backdrop, four major developments shaped the evolution of Palestinian labour and its relation to securing external income for the economy after the creation of the PA. First, Gaza labour lost access to Israeli markets entirely. This occurred gradually. In the period from the

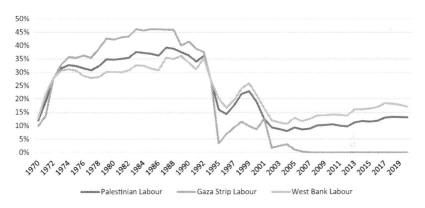

**Fig. 3.3** Percentage of Palestinian labour force employed in Israel, 1970–2020 (*Source* Author's calculations from ICBS [1996] and PCBS [n.d.(a)] data)

signing of the Oslo Accords to 2000, Israeli labour markets relied increasingly on the West Bank's labour force at the expense of Gaza. The Israeli market employed less than 13 per cent of the Gazan labour force by 2000, a substantial drop from 46 per cent in 1990 (ICBS 1996; PCBS, n.d.(a)). After the second Intifada and the beginning of Hamas's control of the Gaza Strip in 2007, the flow of labour from Gaza to Israel ceased entirely (PCBS, n.d.(a)).

The second development that shaped the evolution of labour structure was that Palestinians' ability to access and work in Israel was increasingly restricted after the creation of the PA. New Israeli security policies and restrictions on movement and access measures enforced by the Israeli military impeded the flow of Palestinian labour to Israeli markets (Human Rights Watch 1996). These measures included the completion of Israel's Separation Wall in the West Bank and the erection of more than 705 closure obstacles across the territory (OCHA 2019). Nearly 70 per cent of all West Bank low-skilled labourers were employed in Israel by the end of the 1980s, in contrast to 25 per cent in 2020 (Abu-Shokor 1987; PCBS, n.d.(a)). New Israeli measures dictated that workers must undergo a process of applying for work permits and renewing them every three to six months (Hackl 2017).

The third development shaping Palestinian labour and its relation to external income generation was that, in addition to the sharp decline in the number of Palestinians employed in Israel, other factors such as the rapid increase in population, Israeli economic control policies, and weakness in the Palestinian private sector contributed to a sharp increase in the rate of unemployment, as illustrated in Fig. 3.4. Although unemployment dropped to 12 per cent in 1999, it then rebounded and stabilised at around 25 per cent. The sharp increase in unemployment figures moved in tandem with the percentage of Palestinian labour employed in Israel. For example, unemployment increased from 14 per cent in 2000 to 31 per cent in 2002, while the percentage of Palestinian labour employed in Israel dropped from 23 per cent to nine per cent during the same period. At 47 per cent, the unemployment rate was much higher in the Gaza Strip, where there was zero employment in Israeli markets, than in the West Bank (16 per cent, with 19 per cent of the labour force working in Israel) (PCBS 2022).

The final development shaping the evolution of the labour force and its relation to external income generation was the expansion of public sector employment after the creation of the PA. As Fig. 3.5 illustrates,

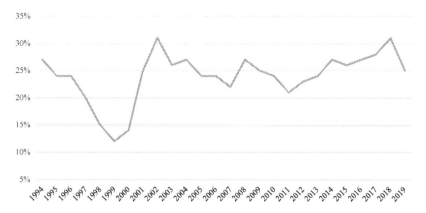

**Fig. 3.4** Percentage of unemployment in Palestine, 1994–2019 (*Source* Author's calculations from World Bank [n.d.(b)] data)

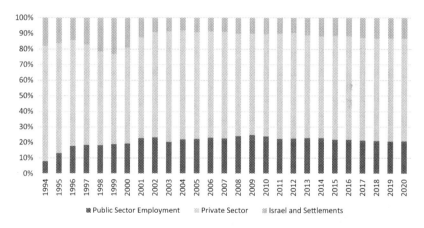

**Fig. 3.5** Labour force distribution in Palestine, 1994–2020 (Calculated from PCBS [n.d.(a)] data)

in 1994 only eight per cent of the labour force was employed by the PA, but this figure increased to 21 per cent in 2020. In contrast, the private sector employed 74 per cent of the overall labour force in 1994 but absorbed only 66 per cent in 2020. The World Bank estimates that between 1994 and 2017, the Palestinian economy needed to create more

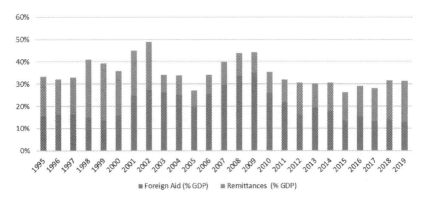

**Fig. 3.6** Rentier income (remittances and foreign aid) as per cent of GDP, 1995–2019 (Calculated from World Bank [n.d.(b)] data)

than 800,000 new jobs just to accommodate new entrants to the labour force, but only created 570,000 jobs (Ridao-Cano et al. 2019). In addition, the public sector accounted for the vast majority of this job creation, at around 300,000 jobs.

These four developments disentangled the long-standing relationship between a sizeable portion of the labour force and the generation of external income. It further resulted in exerting immense pressure on the newly formed PA to expand public employment to accommodate for lost job opportunities in Israeli markets (see Chapter 5). In essence, a significant portion of the labour force shifted from forming the main engine of external income generation to relying on public employment financed by the PA's external income (see Chapters 4 and 5).

In addition to remittances, the West Bank and Gaza received large sums in aid disbursements. Although consistent and complete data on aid delivery modalities, sectoral distribution and providers are sparse, according to the World Bank database more than USD 41 billion in aid was spent in the West Bank and Gaza between 1994 and 2019 (World Bank, n.d.). This translated to an average of USD 422 per capita per year, which consistently placed Palestinians among the highest per capita aid recipients in the world. When compiling remittances and foreign aid data, it becomes clear that the Palestinian economy has developed a severe dependency on external income, and that this dependency accelerated after the creation of the PA. External income relative to GDP, as demonstrated in Fig. 3.6, averaged at around 35 per cent of GDP between 1995 and 2019. This ratio of external income to GDP was high compared with regional rentier states. For example, Saudi Arabia's natural resource rent-to-GDP ratio averaged 36 per cent during the same period, while Qatar's ratio was 32 per cent. Even when taking into account non-traditional rentier states and calculating remittances and foreign aid flows, the Palestinian case remained significantly high relative to regional or comparable states. For example, Jordan's foreign aid and remittances external income relative to GDP for the same period stood at 24 per cent; Lebanon's was 19 per cent and Afghanistan's was 32 per cent.

## 3.4 THE PALESTINIAN AUTHORITY'S BUDGET

Similarly to the Palestinian economy, the PA was over-reliant on external sources of income. While the economy was reliant on foreign aid and remittances, PA finances were contingent upon the flow of clearance revenue and portions of foreign aid in the form of budgetary support. Budgetary support gobbled 46 per cent of all foreign aid disbursed in Palestine between 1994 and 2019. Table 3.2 provide basic data on the PA's budget showcasing the PA's revenues and expenditures in current USD.[1]

The PA began to raise revenues in its own right following its establishment in 1994, and managed to raise revenues equivalent to nine per cent of GDP. This percentage increased after 1996 to consistently count for at least 22 per cent of GDP. However, the PA did not have full control over its revenues, which were divided into two categories. The first was domestic revenue, which derived mostly from indirect taxes on goods and services, some direct taxes on income and corporations, and other non-tax revenues. This category represented revenues that fell under the direct control of the PA and equalled on average 7.8 per cent of GDP, forming 38 per cent of total revenues before foreign aid. The second category of PA revenues was clearance revenue. Clearance revenue formed the bulk of the PA's income, increasing from USD 266 million in 1995 to more than

---

[1] Tables were constructed by the author based on data collected from the IMF, *Report to the Ad Hoc Liaison Committee* (2004–2022); PA Ministry of Finance and Planning, *Financial Reports* (1999–2022); World Bank, *Country Profile: West Bank and Gaza* (n.d.(b)).

**Table 3.2** PA fiscal operations, 1994–2020 (current USD millions)

| | 1994 | 1995 | 1996 | 1997 | 1998 | 1999 | 2000 | 2001 | 2002 | 2003 | 2004 | 2005 | 2006 | 2007 |
|---|---|---|---|---|---|---|---|---|---|---|---|---|---|---|
| NET REVENUES | 269 | 511 | 645 | 807 | 868 | 942 | 939 | 688 | 557 | 762 | 954 | 1232 | 1149 | 1269 |
| Gross Domestic Revenues | 244 | 244 | 294 | 331 | 324 | 362 | 351 | 273 | 215 | 291 | 337 | 476 | 396 | 400 |
| Tax | 132 | 144 | 208 | 213 | 225 | 248 | 241 | 180 | 135 | 167 | 191 | 231 | 239 | 201 |
| Non-tax | 112 | 100 | 86 | 118 | 97 | 114 | 111 | 92 | 80 | 124 | 146 | 245 | 157 | 199 |
| Clearance revenues | 25 | 266 | 352 | 476 | 544 | 580 | 587 | 415 | 342 | 472 | 617 | 757 | 770 | 894 |
| TOTAL EXPENDITURES | ... | ... | 1072 | 1130 | 1075 | 1182 | 1212 | 1117 | 1051 | 1140 | 1528 | 1994 | 2558 | 2638 |
| Recurrent Expenditures | ... | ... | 830 | 868 | 839 | 943 | 1199 | 1098 | 1042 | 1067 | 1353 | 1606 | 2277 | 2507 |
| Gross Wages | ... | ... | 403 | 470 | 467 | 519 | 622 | 678 | 642 | 743 | 870 | 1001 | 1193 | 1280 |
| Nonwage expenditures | ... | ... | 427 | 398 | 372 | 424 | 577 | 417 | 352 | 324 | 465 | 605 | 747 | 693 |
| *of which Transfers* | ... | ... | ... | ... | ... | ... | ... | ... | ... | *201* | ... | ... | ... | ... |
| *of which Net lending* | ... | ... | ... | ... | ... | ... | ... | ... | *0* | *173* | *157* | *344* | *337* | *534* |
| Development Expenditures | ... | ... | 242 | 262 | 236 | 239 | 13 | 22 | 9 | 73 | 175 | 388 | 281 | 131 |
| OVERALL BALANCE | ... | ... | −427 | −323 | −206 | −240 | −274 | −845 | −726 | −531 | −574 | −762 | −1409 | −971 |
| Total Financing | | | | | | | | | | | | | | |
| External Budget Support | ... | ... | 735 | 302 | 239 | 245 | 54 | 530 | 467 | 261 | 353 | 349 | 1022 | 1141 |
| Other Financing | ... | ... | | | | | | 315 | 259 | 270 | 87 | 109 | 147 | −54 |
| *of which arrears (net change)* | ... | ... | *0* | *5* | *74* | *84* | *152* | *361* | *415* | *−115* | ... | ... | *887* | *−23* |
| *of which domestic financing (net)* | ... | ... | *52* | *15* | *−108* | *−15* | *154* | *83* | *134* | | *134* | *304* | *−172* | *−132* |

| | 2008 | 2009 | 2010 | 2011 | 2012 | 2013 | 2014 | 2015 | 2016 | 2017 | 2018 | 2019 | 2020 |
|---|---|---|---|---|---|---|---|---|---|---|---|---|---|
| **NET REVENUES** | **1568** | **1598** | **1883** | **2046** | **2072** | **2312** | **2744** | **2756** | **3457** | **3567** | **3558** | **3474** | **3438** |
| **Gross Domestic Revenues** | 562 | 585 | 701 | 738 | 728 | 853 | 870 | 855 | 1224 | 1154 | 1198 | 1125 | 1103 |
| Tax | 273 | 301 | 431 | 483 | 480 | 597 | 601 | 606 | 623 | 764 | 794 | 767 | 733 |
| Non-tax | 289 | 284 | 270 | 256 | 248 | 255 | 270 | 249 | 601 | 390 | 405 | 358 | 370 |
| Clearance revenues | 1122 | 1103 | 1258 | 1424 | 1457 | 1691 | 2049 | 2055 | 2325 | 2486 | 2432 | 2433 | 2350 |
| **TOTAL EXPENDITURES** | **3273** | **3620** | **3371** | **3695** | **3768** | **3880** | **4330** | **4206** | **4537** | **4737** | **4807** | **4731** | **5099** |
| **Recurrent Expenditures** | 2886 | 3190 | 3073 | 3325 | 3525 | 3693 | 4068 | 3976 | 4202 | 4370 | 4426 | 4071 | 4453 |
| Gross Wages | 1453 | 1467 | 1612 | 1783 | 1767 | 1919 | 2050 | 1914 | 2041 | 2120 | 1957 | 1866 | 2001 |
| Nonwage expenditures | 985 | 1349 | 1226 | 1402 | 1481 | 1564 | 1732 | 1761 | 1893 | 1983 | 2169 | 2206 | 2453 |
| *of which Transfers* | | | | | | | | | *1139* | *1193* | *1348* | *1402* | *1615* |
| *of which Net lending* | *447* | *374* | *236* | *140* | *278* | *210* | *286* | *301* | *268* | *267* | *300* | *319* | *370* |
| **Development Expenditures** | 215 | 430 | 298 | 370 | 243 | 187 | 262 | 230 | 335 | 367 | 381 | 341 | 277 |
| **OVERALL BALANCE** | −1905 | −1771 | −1489 | −1649 | −1696 | −1568 | −1586 | −1450 | −1080 | −1170 | −1249 | −767 | −1199 |
| **Total Financing** | | | | | | | | | | | | | |

(continued)

**Table 3.2** (continued)

| | 2008 | 2009 | 2010 | 2011 | 2012 | 2013 | 2014 | 2015 | 2016 | 2017 | 2018 | 2019 | 2020 |
|---|---|---|---|---|---|---|---|---|---|---|---|---|---|
| External Budget Support | 1979 | 1755 | 1275 | 984 | 930 | 1361 | 1230 | 798 | 760 | 722 | 674 | 498 | 347 |
| Other Financing | −420 | 438 | 194 | 664 | 813 | 206 | 367 | 646 | 316 | 449 | 100 | 722 | 1199 |
| *of which arrears (net change)* | *−387* | *270* | *97* | *571* | *686* | *465* | *493* | *483* | *442* | *352* | *0* | *262* | *626* |
| *of which domestic financing (net)* | *−29* | *176* | *97* | *93* | *127* | *−248* | *−131* | *174* | *−108* | *140* | *100* | *504* | *573* |

*Source* Author's calculations based on data available from the IMF and PA Ministry of Finance and Planning

USD 2.4 billion in 2019 and nearly doubling as a percentage of GDP from 8.1 per cent in 1995 to 14.2 in 2019. Clearance revenue fell under the complete control of the Israeli government and was transferred to the PA on a monthly basis.

Although the PA was often commended for managing to secure a healthy revenue base in its early years, the increase in its revenue base ceased after 2006. In 2003, the IMF noted that the contribution of revenue to GDP was substantially above the average for Arab countries in the region (Toujas-Bernaté 2003). The IMF attributed this to 'the PA's efforts in strengthening its tax administration capabilities, the establishment of the revenue clearance system with Israel and the setting up of mechanisms to mobilise domestic tax revenue' (Toujas-Bernaté 2003, p. 61). However, the PA did not accelerate its revenue mobilisation efforts, and by 2015 its revenue-to-GDP ratio was significantly below the world average, the Middle East and North Africa average, and the average of emerging and developing countries (Economy Watch Data Base, n.d.). The stagnation in revenue mobilisation occurred despite the fact that PA revenues grew on average by 12 per cent annually and increased in value by more than 600 per cent between 1995 and 2019, from USD 511 million to USD 3.5 billion.

The substantial increase in aggregate revenues concealed the fact that the PA revenue base was excessively derived from indirect taxes. Figure 3.7 displays the composition of PA's revenues disaggregated by source for 2017, and shows that only 6 per cent of revenues originated from direct taxes. This includes income accrued from public employment, private sector wages and taxes levied on corporations. On the other hand, indirect taxes, whether originating from clearance revenue or domestic indirect taxes, formed the bulk of revenues at about 84 per cent. Finally, non-tax revenues originating from domestic fees and charges formed about 12 per cent of total revenues. This distribution represents the typical composition of PA revenues since 1995, whereby direct taxes have represented on average less than six per cent of total revenue.

Other than domestic and clearance revenue, the PA received consistent foreign funding in the form of budgetary support. Budgetary support represented nearly half of all foreign aid disbursed in the Palestinian economy between 1995 and 2019. Donors could channel funds in three ways: directly through their respective aid agencies, indirectly via multilateral organisations such as the World Bank or United Nations agencies, or by allocating their funds to the PA's budget. The World Bank, for

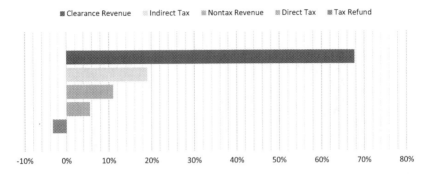

**Fig. 3.7** PA revenue in 2020 (Calculated from data in the Palestinian Ministry of Finance and Planning Quarterly Budgetary Reports 2020)

example, was a major donor to the PA and the wider Palestinian economy, but 80 per cent of its funding consisted of donations from individual countries that were channelled through the bank (Tartir and Wildeman 2016). In addition, the United Nations Relief and Works Agency received more than USD 6 billion in aid between 1993 and 2016 (OECD, n.d.). The PA's budget, however, gobbled at least 46 per cent of all foreign aid disbursed in Palestine. This budgetary support peaked relative to the PA's overall budget in 2008 at 54 per cent and a value of nearly USD 2 billion. On average, foreign aid represented 31 per cent of the PA's total expenditure.

The PA's budget was partitioned into the recurrent budget and the development budget. After the creation of the PA in 1993, donors envisioned that the PA would be able to raise enough domestic revenue to finance its recurrent expenditures, while foreign aid would be devoted to funding long-term investments through the development budget (Adam et al. 2004, p. 64; Iqtait 2021). However, substantial sums of foreign aid channelled through the PA's budget were dedicated to the PA's short-term recurrent expenditures. On average, less than 20 per cent of foreign aid was allocated for developmental expenditures. In this regard, and since 1994 the PA's development budget has been entirely funded by foreign aid.

The preceding discussion on the Palestinian Authority's revenues illuminates the PA's near-total empirical and structural dependence on rentier income. First, 76 per cent of all PA revenue between 1996 and 2020 comprised of rentier income in the form of clearance revenue (45 per cent) or foreign aid (31 per cent). Second, most of the PA's pre-foreign aid revenue originated from economic activity with or through the Israeli economy and remained under Israeli control after the creation of the PA. For example, 67 per cent of the PA's pre-foreign aid revenue was composed of clearance revenue. Similarly, taxes that fell under the direct control of the PA mostly accrued from products that were traded with the Israeli economy (Iqtait 2019). This entailed that, similarly to the situation that preceded the creation of the PA, Israel continued to exercise near-total control over fiscal resources in the West Bank and Gaza. In addition, budgetary support represented another form of external income to the PA. Foreign aid bridged the PA's deficits and financed its development and recurrent expenditures. However, external budgetary support was inconsistent, with disbursements peaking in 2008 at 27 per cent of GDP but declining to three per cent of GDP in 2019.

The PA's dependency on external income was relational. Dependence on clearance revenue and foreign aid implied that the PA could balance the two sources of external income in case of a decline in or suspension of either source. However, the PA's limited political and economic influence in relation to Israel constrained its ability to leverage the realisation of this advantage. In addition, the fragmentation of foreign aid delivery methods, as well as a large number of donors, reduced the reliability of budgetary support in case of clearance revenue suspension (Iqtait 2020).

This can be observed during the periods in which Israel suspended the transfer of clearance revenue to the PA. As Table 3.3 illustrates, between 1994 and 2020 Israel suspended the transfer of clearance revenue to the PA on seven occasions for a cumulative period of five years and five months, during which about USD 4.8 billion was withheld. Each time suspensions occurred the Palestinian economy experienced severe contractions, restricting the PA's ability to fund public expenditure. In most cases, donors were reluctant to fund the resultant deficit in the PA's budget. For example, when clearance revenue transfers were suspended after the PA's application at the United Nations to upgrade Palestine to a member state, the United States, the PA's largest bilateral donor, threatened to withhold aid transfers (Charbonneau and Nichols 2012).

Although foreign aid and clearance revenue were controlled by donors and Israel, the two sources of funding were politically interrelated. On occasions where Israel suspended the transfer of clearance revenue under the pretext of security or political concerns, some donors would similarly respond by limiting aid disbursements (author interview with Ali

**Table 3.3** History of clearance revenue transfer suspensions

| Suspension period | Declared reason | Estimated amounts withheld (in US dollar millions)[a] | Total period (in months) |
|---|---|---|---|
| August to September 1997 | Deterioration in security and political conditions, and bombings in Jerusalem[b] | 87 | 2 |
| December 2000 to December 2002 | The outbreak of the second Intifada in September 2000[c] | 500 | 24 |
| March 2006 to July 2007 | Hamas's electoral victory in Palestinian Legislative Council, and formation of government[d] | 1100 | 16 |
| May 2011 | PA and Hamas national reconciliation agreement | 100 | 1 |
| November 2011 | PA's application at UN to upgrade Palestine to a member state; and UNESCO admission of Palestine[e] | 100 | 1 |
| December 2012 to March 2013 | PA's successful bid at UN General Assembly to upgrade Palestine status to non-member observer state[f] | 400 | 4 |
| December 2014 to April 2015 | Palestine's accession to the Rome Statute of the International Criminal Court[g] | 500 | 5 |
| March 2019 to August 2019 | PA rejected clearance revenue after Israel deducted an amount earmarked for Palestinian prisoners and those killed by Israel | 1100 | 6 |

| Suspension period | Declared reason | Estimated amounts withheld (in US dollar millions)[a] | Total period (in months) |
| --- | --- | --- | --- |
| May 2020 to November 2020 | PA's suspension of cooperation with Israel in response to Israeli pledges to annex parts of the West Bank | 890 | 6 |

[a] Estimates based on the author's calculations from data available from the IMF, UNCTAD and the Palestinian Ministry of Finance and Planning
[b] Kock and Qassis (2012, p. 30)
[c] Ibid.
[d] Ibid.
[e] Ibid.
[f] UNCTAD (2015, p. 6)
[g] Ibid., p. 5

Jarbawi, Birzeit 2017). This occurred after the outbreak of the second Intifada, Hamas's electoral victory in the Palestinian Legislative Council, and the PA's push for statehood recognition in international organisations. Instead of suspending aid transfers on these occasions, some donors resorted to channelling funds away from the PA's budget and through Palestinian NGOs and international aid agencies (author interview with Duaa Qurai, Ramallah 2017). In addition, Arab donors' infrequent and volatile donations further eroded the PA's ability to balance the two sources of rentier income (author interview with Riyadh Mousa, Birzeit 2017).

Although the PA's ability to balance foreign aid and clearance revenue was limited, it actively sought to improve the conditions of its dependence on clearance revenue. This can be observed in the PA's repeated attempts to improve the mechanisms guiding revenue collection and transfers by Israel (Palestine Economic Policy Research Institute [PECRI] 2012). For example, in 2012 PA and Israeli officials reached an agreement that would increase the amount of clearance revenue by changing the calculation methodology from reported to the actual transfer of goods between the two sides (PECRI 2012, p. 9). This step, coming in addition to introducing new technologies to limit tax evasion, was expected to increase clearance revenue by five per cent (PECRI 2012, p. 9).

### 3.4.1 Allocative Expenditure Policy

Chapter 2 theorised that states that rely on rentier income as main sources of revenue are often allocative, rather than extractive, states due to the absence of an effective tax base. They tend to boast large expenditure policies relative to economic activity (GDP) and an inflated public sector. Moreover, the majority of their expenditure is spent on wages or social transfers. Thus, rentier states are fixated on short-term prosperity resulting from the allocation of rents (Luciani 1987, p. 70). Luciani (1987, p. 74) contends that the rentier state 'does not need to formulate anything deserving the appellation of economic policy: all it needs is an expenditure policy'.

In the Palestinian case, the PA's short-term expenditures formed 90 per cent of its total budget. The PA's expenditures were mainly allocative, with 51 per cent dedicated to public sector wages and an additional 25 per cent financing social transfers. When the PA was formed in 1994, public sector employment formed less than eight per cent of total labour force participation. About **20,000** persons were employed by the Israeli military government, mostly teachers and health professionals (ICBS 1996). The following years witnessed a rapid expansion in the number and function of public sector employees (Pannier 1996). By 2020, the PA had an employment pool of about **201,000** staff, with an estimated **81,000** persons employed in the security sector alone (Niksic and Eddin 2016, pp. 11–13; Iqtait 2020). Public employment as a percentage of the labour force increased to more than 25 per cent of the labour force by 2009, although it has since declined to approximately 21 per cent in 2020 (PCBS 2022).

Although the overall size of PA public employment was not large relative to that of other countries, the wage bill associated with public employment was very high. Public sector employment was equivalent to five per cent of the Palestinian population (Niksic and Eddin 2016, p. 14). However, the PA's wage bill ranked as one of the highest in the world as a percentage of GDP and relative to public expenditures. The wage bill represented about 17 per cent of GDP and consumed more than 54 per cent of the recurrent budget; in recent years, the PA was pressured by the IMF and World Bank to reduce its wage bill and in 2013 it implemented a 'zero net hiring' policy and severely limited public wage increases (Niksic and Eddin 2016, pp. 10–13).

While the aggregate levels of public employment were not large, the PA's security sector was overstaffed and consumed large portions of the budget. The wage bill of the security sector alone represented eight per cent of GDP and more than 53 per cent of the total PA wage bill. This percentage was excessive compared to international standards, with most countries allocating 2.0–2.5 per cent of GDP for total military spending in 2013 (i.e., salaries, operating costs, and capital spending of military and paramilitary units). The percentage was also large compared to regional standards; only Saudi Arabia outspent the PA, with a security sector wage bill of 9.2 per cent of GDP, compared to 3.5 per cent in Jordan, and 5.6 per cent in Israel (Niksic and Eddin 2016, p. 15). Furthermore, the PA routinely dedicated more than 27 per cent of its annual expenditures to the security sector. This percentage is considered to be among the highest in the world, second only to Oman at 29.4 per cent and ahead of the Middle East and North Africa regional average of 16 per cent and the world's average of six per cent (Iqtait 2020, p. 97). Similarly, the security sector's wage bill stood at eight per cent of Palestinian GDP, double the regional average of 4.5 per cent (Niksic and Eddin 2016, p. 8).

In addition to salaries, the PA allocated a large share of its budgets to social spending. This category was composed of targeted social assistance programmes, transfers to vulnerable families and unemployment benefits. These transfers represented about 11 per cent of total spending or three per cent of GDP in 2019 About 115,000 households, or 633,000 individuals, benefited from this category. Through this programme, the PA maintained one of the most advanced cash assistance programmes in the Middle East and North Africa (World Bank 2015).

## 3.5 Conclusion

The chapter has demonstrated that while states' revenues and composition play a central role in shaping the construction of the state and its behaviour, other historical, political and external factors play fundamental roles in sculpting the state's final character. This also applies to the wider economic structure and the overall composition of economic activity and employment generation. The chapter highlighted that economic activity and public revenues in the West Bank and Gaza have historically been shaped by Israel's political and economic policies and disproportionately relied on rentier income.

Israel's occupation of the West Bank and Gaza in 1967 shaped the economic conditions. The Israeli military governments' economic policies concentrated on increasing income levels for Palestinians instead of stimulating economic development. As a result, external income from wage earners employed in Israel, or elsewhere, funded a significant portion of economic activity between 1967 and 1993. Transfers of foreign aid provided another source of external income. The lack of economic development spending by the Israeli military governments invited international donors to alleviate the low living standards of the local population. However, most foreign aid was expended on short-term, non-productive projects. Foreign aid was mostly used to fund local consumption and swelled imports, intensifying economic rentier symptoms. Moreover, Israeli policies steered foreign aid disbursements away from productive sectors into humanitarian handouts or basic infrastructural and public works.

The fiscal character before 1994 was also predominantly defined by external income. Although the Israeli military governments did not boast a large budget relative to the size of the Palestinian economy between 1967 and 1993, they funded expenditure policies mainly through custom duties, taxes deducted from Palestinian labour in Israel, and some foreign aid transfers. A significant portion of public services was outsourced to international organisations or local non-governmental organisations. By 1993, the fiscal skeleton of the Israeli military governments' budget was small and heavily reliant on external income and indirect taxes.

Reliance on rentier income increased after the creation of the PA. Although the share of Palestinian labour employed in Israel declined from 40 per cent to less than 12 per cent of the labour force after 1994, their external income remained a significant driver of domestic economic activity. In addition, donors invested more than USD 40 billion in the West Bank and Gaza between 1994 and 2019. Foreign aid funded a series of emergency, ad hoc programmes, most of them carried out by the PA.

After 1994, the PA was tasked with the establishment of a tax apparatus sufficient to fund its operations. However, the PA's revenue generation record remained poor at two levels. The first level reflected the PA's excessive reliance on indirect revenues. About 84 per cent of all revenue accrued to the PA was a result of indirect taxes, with only six per cent from direct taxation. The second level was tied to the PA's reliance on Israel to collect the majority of indirect taxes on its behalf under the clearance revenue mechanism. About 70 per cent of the PA's domestic revenue was collected, processed and transferred by Israel to the PA on a monthly basis.

The PA's finances arising from domestic revenues and clearance revenue amounted to only 60 per cent of its total expenditures. Foreign aid, in the form of budgetary support, bridged some of the gap between PA revenues and expenditures. Foreign aid directly transferred to the PA's budget accounted for nearly 50 per cent of total foreign aid disbursements. Budgetary support formed, on average, 30 per cent of the PA's total expenditures.

As such, this chapter argued that the PA's fiscal structure was largely composed of rentier income. Around 75 per cent of the PA's expenditures were financed by either clearance revenues or foreign aid. In addition, the Palestinian economy was rent-driven, with a rent-to-GDP ratio of 37 per cent. The PA's expenditure policy further confirmed the rentier classification of the PA, with 75 per cent of expenditure dedicated to public sector wages or social transfers.

## REFERENCES

Abu-Shokor, Abdelfattah. 1987. *Socio-economic Conditions of West Bank and Gaza Strip Workers in Israel.* Nablus: An-Najah University.

Adam, Christopher, David Cobham, and Nu'man Kanafani. 2004. 'Budgetary and Fiscal Policy.' In *The Economics of Palestine: Economic Policy and Institutional Reform for a Viable Palestine,* edited by David Cobham and Nu'man Kanafani, 63–89. London: Routledge.

Arnon, Arie, and Avia Spivak. 1996. 'A Seigniorage Perspective on the Introduction of a Palestinian Currency.' *Middle East Business and Economic Review* 8, no. 1: 1–14.

Arnon, Arie, and Jimmy Weinblatt. 2001. 'Sovereignty and Economic Development: The Case of Israel and Palestine.' *The Economic Journal* 111, no. 472: F295–F298295.

Arnon, Arie, Israel Luski, Avia Spivak, and Jimmy Weinblatt. 1997a. 'The Palestinian Economy: A Macroeconomic Profile.' In *The Palestinian Economy: Between Imposed Integration and Voluntary Separation,* edited by Arie Arnon, Israel Luski, Avia Spivak, and Jimmy Weinblatt, 12–60. Leiden: Brill.

Arnon, Arie, Israel Luski, Avia Spivak, and Jimmy Weinblatt, eds. 1997b. *The Palestinian Economy: Between Imposed Integration and Voluntary Separation.* Leiden: Brill.

Arnon, Arie, Israel Luski, Avia Spivak, and Jimmy Weinblatt. 1997c. 'The Public Sector.' In *The Palestinian Economy: Between Imposed Integration and Voluntary Separation,* edited by Arie Arnon, Israel Luski, Avia Spivak and Jimmy Weinblatt, 136–37. Leiden: Brill.

Baxendale, Sidney. 1989. 'Taxation of Income in Israel and the West Bank: A Comparative Study.' *Journal of Palestine Studies* 18, no. 3: 134–41.

Beblawi, Hazem. 1987. 'The Rentier State in the Arab World.' In *The Rentier State: Nation, State and the Integration of the Arab World,* edited by Hazem Beblawi and Giacomo Luciani, Chapter 2. London: Croom Helm.

Benvenisti, Meron. 1987. *Demographic, Economic, Legal, Social and Political Developments in the West Bank.* Jerusalem: The Jerusalem Post.

Bregman, Ahron. 2014. *Cursed Victory: A History of Israel and the Occupied Territories.* London: Penguin.

Charbonneau, Louis, and Michelle Nichols. 2012. 'Palestinians Win De Facto U.N. Recognition of Sovereign State.' *Reuters,* December 1. https://reut.rs/2FjSFsg.

Cobban, Helena. 1990. 'The PLO and the "Intifada".' *Middle East Journal* 44, no. 2: 222.

Committee on Foreign Affairs. 1979. *Economic Support Funds Programme in the Middle East.* Washington, DC: United States Congress.

Cowell, Alan. 1989. 'Beit Sahur Journal: In a Tax War, Even the Olivewood Dove Is Seized.' *The New York Times*, October 11. https://www.nytimes.com/1989/10/11/world/beit-sahur-journal-in-a-tax-war-even-the-olivewood-dove-is-seized.html.

Diwan, Ishac, and Radwan Shaban. 1999. *Development Under Adversity? The Palestinian Economy in Transition.* Washington, DC: Palestine Economic Policy Research and the World Bank.

Economy Watch Data Base. n.d. General Government Revenue (% of GDP) Data for All Countries. http://www.economywatch.com/economic-statistics/economic-indicators/General_Government_Revenue_Percentage_GDP/.

Gazit, Shlomo. 1995. *The Carrot and the Stick: Israel's Policy in Judea and Samaria, 1967–1968.* Washington, DC: B'nai B'rith Books.

General Secretariat of the Joint Committee. 1987. *Report of Achievement 1979–1986.* Joint Jordanian–Palestinian Committee to Support the Steadfastness of the Palestinian People in the Occupied Homeland.

Gharaibeh, Fawazi. 1985. *The Economies of the West Bank and Gaza Strip.* London: Westview Press.

Hackl, Andreas. 2017. 'Occupied Labour: The Treadmill of Palestinian Work in Israel.' *IRIN*. https://www.refworld.org/docid/59883e304.html.

Hamed, Osama, and Radwan Shaban. 1994. 'One-Sided Customs and Monetary Union: The Case of the West Bank and Gaza Strip under Israeli Occupation.' In *The Economics of Middle East Peace: Views from the Region*, edited by Stanley Fischer, Dani Rodrik, and Elias Tuma, 117–48. Cambridge, MA: MIT Press.

Hiltermann, Joost. 1991. *Behind the Intifada: Labor and Women's Movements in the Occupied Territories.* Princeton, NJ: Princeton University Press.

Human Rights Watch. 1996. 'Israel's Closure of the West Bank and Gaza Strip.' Human Rights Watch 8, no. 3.

Iqtait, Anas. 2019. 'The Political Economy of Taming the Palestinian Authority.' In *Palestine: Past and Present*, edited by Tristan Dunning, 145–75. Nova Publishing.

Iqtait, Anas. 2020. 'The Political Economy of Rentierism of the Palestinian Authority.' PhD diss., The Australian National University.

Iqtait, Anas. 2021. 'The Palestinian Authority Political Economy: The Architecture of Fiscal Control.' In *Political Economy of Palestine*, edited by Alaa Tartir et al., 249–70. Cham: Palgrave Macmillan.

Israeli Central Bureau of Statistics (ICBS). 1996. *National Accounts of Judea, Samaria and the Gaza Area 1968–1993.* Jerusalem: ICBS.

Jenkins, J. Craig, Katherine Meyer, Matthew Costello, and Hassan Aly. 2011. 'International Rentierism in the Middle East and North Africa, 1971–2008.' *International Area Studies Review* 14, no. 3: 3–31.

68 A. IQTAIT

Khouri, Rami. 1980. 'Israel's Imperial Economics.' *Journal of Palestine Studies* 9, no. 2: 71–78.

Kock, Udom, and Hania Qassis. 2012. *Recent Experience and Prospects of the Economy of the West Bank and Gaza.* International Monetary Fund.

Luciani, Giacomo. 1987. 'Allocation Vs. Production States.' In *The Rentier State: Nation, State and the Integration of the Arab World*, edited by Hazem Beblawi and Giacomo Luciani, 64–80. London: Croom Helm.

Mansour, Antoine. 1988. 'The West Bank Economy: 1948–1984.' In *The Palestinian Economy*, edited by George Abed, 81–82. London: Routledge.

Moore, Mick. 2004. 'Revenues, State Formation, and the Quality of Governance in Developing Countries.' *International Political Science Review* 25, no. 3: 299–305.

Nakhleh, Khalil. 1989. 'Non-Governmental Organizations and Palestine: The Politics of Money.' *Journal of Refugee Studies* 2, no. 1: 113–24.

Newman, Peter. 1984. 'Palestinian Education, A Road to Nowhere?' *Middle East International.* September: 13.

Niksic, Orhan, and Nur Nasser Eddin. 2016. *Palestinian Territories Public Expenditure Review 2013–2014: Towards Enhanced Public Finance Management and Improved Fiscal Sustainability.* Washington, DC: World Bank Group.

Organisation for Economic Co-operation and Develoment (OECD). n.d. *Aid (ODA) Disbursements to Countries and Regions.* https://stats.oecd.org/Index.aspx?datasetcode=TABLE2A.

Palestine Economic Policy Research Institute. 2012. *Recent Amendments to Trade Arrangements in Paris Protocol.* Round Table Discussion 7. Ramallah: PECRI.

Palestinian Central Bureau of Statistics (PCBS). n.d.(a). *Palestinian Labour Force Survey: Annual Report.* https://www.pcbs.gov.ps/site/lang__en/946/default.aspx.

Palestinian Central Bureau of Statistics (PCBS). n.d.(b). *National Accounts Variables in Palestine for the Years 1994–2020 at Current Prices.* http://www.pcbs.gov.ps/site/lang__en/741/default.aspx.

Palestinian Central Bureau of Statistics. 2022. Palestinian Labour Force Survey: Annual Report: 2021. Ramallah—Palestine. https://www.pcbs.gov.ps/Downloads/book2605.pdf.

Pannier, Dominique. 1996. *West Bank and Gaza Civil Service Study, Presentation and Technical Assistance Supervision.* World Bank Memorandum. Washington, DC: World Bank.

Richter, Thomas, and Christian Steiner. 2008. 'Politics, Economics and Tourism Development in Egypt: Insights into the Sectoral Transformations of a Neopatrimonial Rentier State.' *Third World Quarterly* 29, no. 5: 943–44.

Ridao-Cano, Cristobal, Friederike Rother, and Javier Sanchez-Reaza. 2019. *West Bank and Gaza—Jobs in West Bank and Gaza Project: Enhancing Job Opportunities for Palestinians.* Washington, DC: World Bank.

Roy, Sara. 1991. 'Development under Occupation? The Political Economy of US Aid to the West Bank and Gaza Strip.' *Arab Studies Quarterly* 13, no. 3/4: 65–89.

Roy, Sara. 1995. *The Gaza Strip: The Political Economy of De-Development.* Washington, DC: Institute of Palestine Studies.

Roy, Sara. 1998. 'The Palestinian Economy after Oslo.' *Current History* 97, no. 615: 19–25.

Roy, Sara. 1999. 'De-development Revisited: Palestinian Economy and Society since Oslo.' *Journal of Palestine Studies* 28, no. 3: 67–68.

Samara, Adel. 2000. 'Globalization, the Palestinian Economy, and the "Peace Process".' *Journal of Palestine Studies* 29, no. 2: 20–34.

Tartir, Alaa, and Jeremy Wildeman. 2016. 'Mapping of Donor Funding to the Occupied Palestinian Territories 2012-2014/5.' *Aid Watch Palestine*, November. https://alaatartir.com/2017/11/10/mapping-of-donor-funding-to-the-occupied-palestinian-territories-2012-2014-15/.

Toujas-Bernaté, Joel. 2003. *West Bank and Gaza: Economic Performance and Reform Under Conflict Conditions.* Washington, DC: International Monetary Fund.

United Nations Conference on Trade and Development (UNCTAD). 2015. *Report on UNCTAD Assistance to the Palestinian People: Developments in the Economy of the Occupied Palestinian Territory.* Geneva: UNCTAD. https://unctad.org/en/PublicationsLibrary/tdb62d3_en.pdf.

United Nations Office for the Coordination of Humanitarian Affairs (OCHA). 2019. *Occupied Palestinian Territory Humanitarian Atlas*, 4. Jerusalem: United Nations. https://www.ochaopt.org/atlas2019/.

World Bank. 1993. *Developing the Occupied Territories: An Investment in Peace: Overview* (English). Washington, DC: World Bank Group. http://documents.worldbank.org/curated/en/869901468780572753/Overview.

World Bank. 2015. *Palestinian Reform and Development Plan—Trust Fund (PRDP-TF): First Quarterly Review Update.* Working Paper 106076. Washington, DC: World Bank.

World Bank. n.d.(a). Personal Remittances, received (% of GDP). https://data.worldbank.org/indicator/BX.TRF.PWKR.DT.GD.ZS.

World Bank. n.d.(b). *West Bank and Gaza.* https://data.worldbank.org/country/west-bank-and-gaza.

CHAPTER 4

# The Palestinian Authority's Economy of Dual Rentierism

**Abstract** This chapter examines the economic and fiscal effects of external income on the Palestinian economy and the Palestinian Authority since 1994. External income is shown to have resulted in weak and rent-contingent growth and contributed to the erosion of the productive base in the economy and lack of economic diversification. Donors' provision of foreign aid and technical assistance expanded the PA's tax base and developed new tax systems and policies. However, these taxes fell under the direct control of the Israeli government through the clearance revenue mechanism. The mechanism affected the PA in ways that hindered its ability to further expand its tax base and marginalised its role in the importation process from Israel and the rest of the world, which accounted for a large portion of total economic activity. The chapter concludes by demonstrating the PA's attempts at developing fiscal policies linked to the availability of external income.

**Keywords** Paris Protocol · Dutch Disease · Rentier paradox · Taxation · Rentier trap · Fiscal policy

© The Author(s), under exclusive license to Springer Nature Switzerland AG 2023
A. Iqtait, *Funding and the Quest for Sovereignty in Palestine*,
https://doi.org/10.1007/978-3-031-19478-8_4

## 4.1 Introduction

There was a time when some observers thought the Oslo peace process of 1993 would transform the Palestinian economy, creating a modern neoliberal economic oasis of stability and prosperity.[1] Instead, as this chapter will illustrate, the peace process proved detrimental to the Palestinian economy. Israeli and donor-driven policies of development through external income yielded very little success and perpetuated the structural deficiencies that existed due to the high dependency on external income before 1993.

The effects of external income on the Palestinian economy after 1994 were significant in two areas. First, external income in the form of foreign aid and remittances resulted in weak and rent-contingent growth. Second, external income contributed to the erosion of the productive base in the economy and a lack of economic diversification. These exacerbated the Dutch Disease symptoms present in the Palestinian economy before 1993. With the wider economy dependent on external income, the PA also relied on foreign aid and clearance revenue for continuity. Financial and technical assistance from donors helped expand the PA's tax base and develop new tax systems and policies. However, these taxes fell under the direct control of the Israeli government through the clearance revenue mechanism, limiting the PA's ability to further expand its tax base and marginalising its role in the importation process from Israel and the rest of the world, which accounted for a large portion of total economic activity.

This chapter investigates the economic and fiscal consequences of the PA's dual rentierism. It first details the Paris Protocol, the Israeli and donor-driven policy guiding the PA's economic and fiscal relations with Israel and the rest of the world. It then investigates how external income affected economic growth, productive economic capacity, economic diversification, and the presence of the Dutch Disease. It also studies the effect of external income on the PA's taxation and economic and fiscal policies. Finally, the chapter discusses the presence of a 'rentier trap' for the Palestinian economy that perpetuates the PA's reliance on external income in order to sustain its fiscal expenditures.

---

[1] During the Oslo Process between 1994 and 2000, Palestinian officials touted the idea of making Palestine the 'Singapore of the Middle East' (New York Times 1988; Hassan 2011, p. 71; BBC 2001).

## 4.2 THE PARIS PROTOCOL

Economic ties between the Palestinian and Israeli markets after 1993 were shaped by the policy parameters of the Oslo Accords, which instituted a legal framework for Palestinian economic activities and economic relations with Israel and the rest of the world. The Paris Protocol, formally known as the 'Protocol on Economic Relations', was a 'contractual agreement' that governed economic and fiscal relations in the West Bank and Gaza (*Protocol on Economic Relations between the State of Israel and the PLO* ['Paris Protocol'], 1994, Article I). It was concluded in Paris in 1994 as part of the Oslo process between the government of the State of Israel and the PLO, representing the Palestinian people. It meant to 'lay the groundwork for strengthening the economic base of the Palestinian side and for exercising its right of economic decision making in accordance with its own development plan and priorities' (Article I). The Protocol regulated matters related to trade, monetary and financial issues, taxation, labour, agriculture, industry, tourism, and insurance issues. It was designed to serve for an interim period of five years during the 1994–1999 Oslo process but continued to dictate economic and fiscal relations between the PA and Israel after the end of the Oslo process (Article I).

The agreement aimed to institute a customs union between the PA and Israel by officially extending the Israeli trade regime to the West Bank and Gaza. Accordingly, the PA had to apply the same level of customs and other duties as Israel on most imported goods. In return, the Protocol granted Palestinian goods free access to the Israeli market. Agricultural and industrial products were also meant to flow freely between the two sides (Articles IX and X). International tourism was regulated in a manner that allowed Palestinians to control tourist sites in some areas in the West Bank and Gaza and benefit from tourists' movements between the two sides. In addition, the agreement facilitated the access of Palestinian goods to markets of countries with which Israel maintained free-trade agreements, such as Canada, the EU, Turkey, and the USA. But the Protocol reserved for Israel the right to unilaterally determine common external tariffs and trade policies with third countries (Article III).

The agreement stripped the PA of its ability to collect customs revenues on imports from or through Israel. It established that Israel would collect custom taxes, VAT, and excise duties (collectively, clearance revenue) on behalf of the PA. The PA would only receive import taxes and levies based on the principle of the place of final destination on goods marked explicitly for the West Bank and Gaza markets. Clearance revenue funds would be settled and transferred between the two sides on a monthly basis, after Israel deducted a three per cent fee for administrative and handling costs. The Paris Protocol further obliged the PA to fix VAT at a rate close to that of Israel, at 15 or 16 per cent, on all locally produced goods and services and all imports destined to the West Bank and Gaza (Article III).

The central issue of Palestinian labour flows to Israel was addressed in Article VII, which states: 'Both sides will attempt to maintain the normality of movement of labour between them, subject to each side's right to determine from time to time the extent and conditions of the labour movement into its area'. The Protocol remained ambiguous with regard to actual policies for facilitating labour flows to Israeli markets. It focused, instead, on issues pertaining to financial deductions from labour wages in the form of income taxes and social security contributions, and the conditions shaping the transfer of these deductions to the PA (Article VIII).

The Protocol envisioned fostering favourable conditions for the development of the Palestinian economy by binding its trajectory to the well-developed and comparatively wealthy economy of Israel (author interview with Mahmoud Eljafari, Professor of Economics et al.-Quds University, Ramallah, 2020). The continuation of labour movement to Israel and favourable public and private investment conditions could have generated full employment. The public sector could have been developed and a viable tax system established. Foreign aid could have assisted in financing lacking infrastructure and spurred private sector development. Finally, free trade with Israel and access to international markets were projected to boost growth (Arnon and Weinblatt 2001; Kanafani 2001).

However, there was widespread criticism among policy-makers and academics concerning the negative impacts of the Paris Protocol on the Palestinian economy (see, e.g., Roy 2007; Koldas 2017; Samhouri 2016). Most arguments highlighted the asymmetrical relationship between the PA and Israel. The Paris Protocol adopted a liberal 'peace-time' economic framework of the form common among economies of similar economic development levels, and possessing individual sovereignty (Terme and Kattan 2010). The Palestinian economy, however, was in reality characterised by under-development, dependence, and fragmentation. The economy's dependence on that of Israel was a by-product of Israeli economic policies since 1967 and can be best described by the multi-structural sectoral dependence on 'international trade, means of production, labour flows, productivity, fiscal revenues, and energy supplies' (author interview with Fadi Kattan, Dear of Business Administration at Bethlehem University, Bethlehem, 2020). The Paris Protocol instituted the components of the PA's fiscal dependence on Israeli-controlled clearance revenue. As previously demonstrated, the Israeli market absorbs at least 14 per cent of the Palestinian labour force, and historical records highlight that as much as 40 per cent of the entire Palestinian labour force was once employed in Israel (ICBS 1993; PCBS 2022). Further, Israel was the biggest trading partner of the Palestinian economy, with at least 81 per cent of Palestinian exports moving to, and 55 per cent of imports originating from, Israel in 2019 (PCBS 2020). Fiscal revenues from international trade, trade with the Israeli market, and energy purchases through Israel represented the largest share of the clearance revenue mechanism introduced by the Paris Protocol, granting Israel de facto control over the PA's largest source of fiscal revenue.

At the structural level, the PA inherited the fiscal revenue mechanisms implemented by the Israeli military governments prior to 1993. As a result, the external skeleton of PA fiscal resources was largely similar to the mechanisms operating under the Israeli civil administration. In fact, the majority of domestic recoverable fiscal revenue, in the form of fees and corporate taxation, not only remained structurally similar, but Israel also continued to extract and process custom clearance revenue on imports destined for Palestinian consumption, in addition to the revenue withheld from Palestinian labourers in Israel. Furthermore, the fiscal revenue's external composition was nearly identical to that existing under the Israeli civil administration, with 60 per cent of revenue raised by the PA coming from indirect taxation and international trade. From a technical perspective, the clearance revenue mechanism was an intuitive approach to provide the PA with necessary fiscal capital while bypassing the lack of sovereignty offered in the Oslo Accords. The mechanism allowed for the institutionalisation of the political and economic governance mechanisms evolved by the Israeli Defence Ministry, under the PA's management. As a senior Palestinian official noted: 'Nothing in the clearance revenue mechanism or any of the subsequent economic agreements between the PA and Israel indicates economic independence for the Palestinians' (author interview with PA Official, Ramallah, 2017). In this regard, clearance revenue

## 76  A. IQTAIT

was to be entirely controlled and processed by the Israeli side on behalf of the PA, without any mention of future options for the PA to control the collection or processing of these revenues.

### 4.3 DUTCH DISEASE AND THE RENTIER PARADOX

As the Paris Protocol became the de jure regime in 1994, it became clear that economic conditions were largely contingent on the wider political context. The Palestinian economy remained dependent on external sources of income in the form of remittances and foreign aid. This dependence perpetuated several economic consequences that distorted the Palestinian economy. These consequences included weak and rent-dependent growth, the erosion of the productive base in the economy and lack of economic diversification (Dutch Disease). Palestinian dependence on external income precedes the creation of the PA. The share of total external income in the form of remittances and foreign aid from the local economy in the West Bank and Gaza between 1968 and 1993 averaged 29 per cent of GNP (ICBS 1993). External income during this period financed large increases in local consumption and imports. For example, in 1989 private consumption formed more than 80 per cent of GNP and imports stood at 50 per cent (ICBS 1993). By 1993, the productive segments of the economy were under-developed; the services sector was large relative to the agricultural and manufacturing sectors; and economic growth was inconsistent and driven by the availability of external income. Petri described the topography of the Palestinian economy in the early 1990s:

> An especially dramatic example of the Dutch Disease at work is provided by the structure of the Palestinian economy in the early 1990s. Despite its very small economic size, the West Bank and Gaza exported only 14 per cent of its output. These exports paid for only one-fifth of imports, with the remaining 80 per cent financed [externally] by wages earned in Israel. As a result, the [West Bank and Gaza]'s productive resources at home were engaged mostly in non-traded sectors, with tradables accounting for only 8 per cent of output. Nevertheless, wage rates were higher than those in neighbouring Jordan or Egypt. (Petri 1997, p. 25)

The data for 1994–2020 demonstrate that standards of living in the West Bank and Gaza stagnated. This is reflected in national accounts by slow

4 THE PALESTINIAN AUTHORITY'S ECONOMY OF DUAL ... 77

and inconsistent economic growth, decline in aggregate demand levels, and weak per capita growth in economic output and income. Although national income grew by more than 560 per cent between 1994 and 2020, per capita income increased by less than 240 per cent. The excessive presence of external income further contributed to the erosion of the economy's domestic productive capacity. The gap between local economic productive capacity, represented by GDP, and available disposable income, represented by gross national disposable income (GNDI), widened significantly.[2] GNDI exceeded GDP by a significant margin, peaking at 58 per cent in 2008 and averaging 29 per cent between 1994 and 2020. These figures represent one of the highest differentials in the Middle East and North Africa region. They indicate that available income for consumption in the economy far exceeded the available economic resources. As such, 97 per cent of all disposable income was expended on consumption and only three per cent was allocated to overall savings. This consumption fuelled a large trade deficit, with exports at only 29 per cent of imports and the economy exporting a mere 17 per cent of its output (PCBS, n.d.).

The Dutch Disease symptoms can also be observed in the sectoral composition of the Palestinian productive economy. Industrial capacity regressed from 21 per cent of GDP in 1995 to 13 per cent in 2019. This regression was uniform in the West Bank and Gaza, as disaggregated figures indicate similar decline levels. Accompanying this drop in productive capacity was a structural reorientation towards the services sectors. Services' share of GDP increased by more than 10 per cent between 1995 and 2019. In Gaza, this rate was even higher, at 20 per cent. The majority of increase in the services sector was due to accelerated employment and expenditures in the public administration and security sectors (Ridao-Cano et al. 2019). Between 1995 and 2019, the industrial and agricultural sectors shrank by 40 and 70 per cent, respectively, while the services sector increased by 20 per cent. These data indicate that the productive resources of the economy were predominantly engaged in

---

[2] Gross national disposable income (GNDI) is a more accurate method for quantifying the Palestinian economy as explained by Mansour (1988, p. 77): 'Indicators such as GNP, per capita GNP, rates of investment, are not appropriate measures of the strength or weakness of the West Bank economy. These production linked concepts, which are devised to study productive economies, have little significance in economies dominated by transferred resources. The West Bank enjoys an income disproportionate to its productive capabilities.' Therefore, measures such as GNI or GDI are more appropriate for measuring size and strength of the Palestinian economy. See also Chatelus and Schemeil (1984).

non-traded sectors, a prominent feature of the Dutch Disease. Furthermore, the contribution of agriculture and food processing of total credit to the private sector stood at only two per cent, and the mining and manufacturing sectors equalled only six per cent (Ahern 2017, pp. 14–15; Shikaki 2021, pp. 59–63). In contrast, non-productive credit—in the form of basic consumption, car and vehicle finance, and real-estate accounted—formed 60 per cent of total credit. This distribution of credit to the private sector further showcases the weakness of the tradable goods sector and affirms the lack of economic diversification and erosion of productive capacity.

In addition to the Dutch Disease, there is general agreement among researchers that foreign aid failed to achieve any sustainable economic development in Palestine (Barghouti 2011; Hanieh 2016, p. 35; Ibrahim and Beaudet 2012, p. 496; Khalidi and Samour 2011, p. 10; Le More 2010, p. 10; Roy 1999, p. 69). The main goal of donors, as detailed by the World Bank, was to increase the economic standing of ordinary Palestinians in order to foster and support the peace process (World Bank 1993). However, rising unemployment levels, increasing poverty, declining per capita income, continuing de-development of productive sectors in the economy, erratic economic growth rates, increasing public and private debt levels, declining working conditions, rising costs of living, low investment levels, and persistent food insecurity were key socioeconomic indicators of foreign aid's failure in Palestine (Le More 2010; Palestine Economic Policy Research Institute 2012; OCHA 2012; Tartir and Wildeman 2012; Bisn Center 2011; Barghouti 2011; Farsakh 2002). Donors' fixation on increasing income levels without promoting genuine economic development was comparable to the Israeli government's economic policy of increasing income levels through labour remittances. Both policies, foreign aid, and remittances, created a rentier paradox: the only way for the Palestinian economy to grow and achieve higher income levels was through the injection of higher transfers of foreign aid and remittances, but this infusion of rentier income perpetuated the erosion of economic productivity in the economy, thereby increasing its current and future economic dependence.

While the proponents of the Paris Protocol hoped for sustainable economic growth in the Palestinian economy after 1994, the data reflect economic stagnation and limited growth. The rentier conditions the PA inherited in 1993 were accentuated and entrenched. The economy exhibited severe symptoms of the Dutch Disease. External income provided much-needed reserves to finance high import levels needed to compensate for the continuing erosion of the economy's productive capacity in the agricultural and manufacturing sectors (World Bank 2017). The Protocol provided little economic benefit to Palestinians and accelerated Palestinian reliance on rentier income. It also drew the legal and administrative boundaries that would make the PA's fiscal structure to be perpetually dependent on rents (Iqtait 2019).

## 4.4 Rentier Income and PA Taxation

Between 1996 and 2020, the PA had direct control over only 24 per cent of its revenues. The other 76 per cent was controlled by Israel in the form of clearance revenue (45 per cent) and by donors in the form of foreign aid (31 per cent). The revenue under the PA's control accrued partly from tax sources, such as VAT, excises on beverages and tobacco, property taxes, and income tax. The remaining revenue accrued from domestic fees and charges. At the domestic level, Israel's occupation, the PA's lack of sovereignty, and low levels of development were some of the frequently cited circumstances that made it difficult for the PA to tax the economy. Moreover, the proliferation of the services sector facilitated the rise of a large informal economy, further hindering the PA's ability to monitor or formalise tax collection (author interview with Fadi Kattan, Bethlehem 2017).

A small tax base also contributed to this low level of domestic tax collection. According to the Ministry of Finance and Planning, only 30 per cent of the tax base in the West Bank and Gaza Strip was covered (World Bank 2016). A very large number of individuals and businesses were not registered to pay taxes. For example, there were more than 5000 operating businesses in the Governorate of Bethlehem in 2016, but only 1282 were registered with the Bethlehem Chamber of Commerce, and fewer than 50 per cent of registered businesses had ever paid taxes to the PA (author interview with Chamber of Commerce Representative, Bethlehem, 2017). Several studies conducted by domestic and international organisations estimate the value of tax evasion as between 30 and 65 per cent of current tax revenue (Coalition for Transparency and Integrity [CTI] 2017, pp. 4–5).

Weak follow-up procedures on taxpayers, fragile monitoring of unregistered taxpayers, and the absence of field inspections were some of the obstacles hindering the expansion of the tax base and encouraging tax

80 A. IQTAIT

evasion (CTI 2017; author interviews, Ramallah, 2017). Feeble communication and coordination between different tax departments also undermined the PA's revenue performance. Moreover, the lack of professional training for tax directorate employees and shortages of necessary infrastructures, such as efficient computer systems and tax offices, impeded the performance of PA employees. It was common for taxpayers to report long waiting times and unprofessional conduct (in the form of nepotism and personal relationships) by tax directorate staff (author interviews, Ramallah, 2017 and 2020).

A major deterrent to the improvement of tax performance was the lack of motivation among PA officials to raise taxes domestically. Domestic taxation was unpopular with the general public and attainment of an independent state seems to be a prerequisite for the public's readiness to pay taxes. Several PA officials seemed to conform to this view. A senior PA official asserted that 'domestic taxation before realising statehood was not an issue of discussion among PA governments' (author interview with PA official, Ramallah, 2017 and 2020). Another Ministry of Finance and Planning official compared the financial burden of the Israeli occupation to daily taxes, adding 'the pressures of daily struggle for jobs, high prices, and inability to travel freely is enough and enforcing and levying taxes from people would just cause more suffering' (author interview with Ministry of Finance and Planning official, Ramallah, 2017. This view was also shared by another PA official, who stated that 'business owners already face inflated costs for competition with their Israeli counterparts and collecting taxes on their operations would impede their ability to compete and survive' (author interview with PA official, Ramallah 2017).

This position was also reflected in the PA's lax income tax system. Income Tax Law Number 8 of 2011 stated that companies and businesses are subject to a corporate income tax rate of 15 per cent. Individual income tax rates fell into three progressive categories of five, 10, and 15 per cent. Accordingly, the first ILS 75,000 (equivalent to USD 21,000 in 2016) was taxed at five per cent; income between ILS 75,000 and ILS 150,000 was taxed at 10 per cent; and income that exceeded ILS 150,001 was taxed at 15 per cent (Palestinian Investment Promotion Agency, n.d.). Although these individual and corporate tax rates were low relative to regional or international standards, the rate of compliance with tax collection remained poor. Only 1.7 per cent of the PA's revenue accrued from individual income taxes and 2.8 per cent was collected from corporate income taxes in 2016 (World Bank 2016). According to the

IMF, income tax collection (personal and corporate) in 2020 was 1.2 per cent of GDP, which is low compared to other countries at a similar stage of development (IMF 2022).

Securing and mobilising clearance revenue and foreign aid was more efficient and rewarding than expanding the domestic tax base. Many PA officials did not seem to mind the increasing reliance of the PA on clearance revenue: 'clearance revenue is entirely controlled by Israel because we do not have control over our borders. Once a state is declared this revenue will flow directly from Palestinians to the PA' (author interview with PA official, Ramallah, 2017 and 2020). However, the PA's poor domestic tax collection record suggests that the PA would probably be unable to match the current levels of revenue. Eljafari suggests that the PA has had a vested interest in maintaining the status quo of reliance on clearance revenue and foreign aid (author interview with Mahmoud Eljafari, Ramallah, 2017). In particular, while the PA's progress in developing its domestic tax collection record has been unsuccessful, its ability to recover higher sums of clearance revenue developed efficiently. 'The PA has had an active policy of reliance on clearance revenue relative to other forms of revenue or funding', averred a PA senior official, while stressing that this is the only option 'possible' for the PA (author interview with PA official, Ramallah, 2017 and 2020).

Foreign aid was also a top priority for the PA and affected its ability to mobilise local taxation. While many of the tax collection directorates are inadequately funded and understaffed, the Ministry of Finance and Planning invested heavily in hiring qualified individuals to work with donors at the Directorate of International Relations and Projects. The directorate's mission was to work directly with current and potential donors to maintain foreign aid disbursement levels or secure new sources. Ensuring that disbursements were channelled through the PA's budget was also a major responsibility of the directorate (author interview with Ministry of Finance and Planning official, Ramallah, 2017). This dichotomy between the domestic and international Ministry directorates undermined the PA's credibility with its own staff. A tax collection employee of the Ministry explained that the Directorate of International Relations and Projects staff collected their salaries in US dollars while other staff received lower salaries in Israeli shekels (author interview with PA tax collection employee, Ramallah, 2017). Other interviewees also expressed their dissatisfaction with the salary differentials and blamed the PA's fixation on

82    A. IQTAIT

donor funding for the low-quality tax collection services provided to the wider public (author interviews with three PA tax collection employees, West Bank, 2017).

Overall, the PA's rentierism clearly affected its tax collection record. In the words of a former PA minister, '[t]he PA, in its composition and relation with third parties, was established in the West Bank and Gaza Strip as a rentier authority. It then created a relationship with Palestinians defined by their dependence on the state, and not the state's dependence on Palestinians' (interview Ali Jarbawi, former PA minister, Birzeit 2017).

### 4.4.1   PA Taxation and the Clearance Revenue Mechanism

Clearance revenue reflected the economic interconnectedness of the Palestinian and Israeli markets and the economy's excessive reliance on imports. Imports equalled 53 per cent of GDP in 2019 and were 3.4 times greater than exports (PCBS, n.d.). The PCBS estimated that 55 per cent of total imports and 81 per cent of total exports were traded with the Israeli economy (PCBS, n.d.). The value of this trade equalled USD 4.5 billion and included the importation of energy, water, services and basic consumption commodities (PCBS 2020). Clearance revenue captured this activity, in the form of VAT and petroleum excises that represented nearly 55 per cent of total clearance revenue accruing to the PA. The VAT component comprised indirect taxes collected from Palestinian traders' purchases in Israel or on imports. Petroleum excises comprised taxes collected on the purchase of fuel from Israel. The other major component of clearance revenue, as illustrated in Fig. 4.1, was customs. Customs revenues were tariffs collected by Israeli authorities on goods destined for the Palestinian markets and represented 43 per cent of the total revenue accruing to the PA through the clearance revenue mechanism in 2019.

The clearance revenue mechanism affected the PA in five ways. First, the mechanism marginalised the role of the PA in the importation process. Palestinian traders dealt almost exclusively with the Israeli authorities for processing imports to the Palestinian markets, whether they originated from Israel or from the rest of the world. Palestinian traders were not required to possess any licences from the PA in order to trade with the Israeli market. For importing products from the rest of the world, a simple 'import licence' was the only required procedural interaction between the PA and traders. Most interactions were carried out directly with Israeli authorities or Israeli intermediaries, or specialised Israeli clearance and

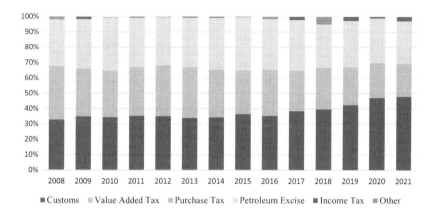

**Fig. 4.1** Clearance revenue composition, 2008–2021 (*Source* Calculated from data in the Ministry of Finance and Planning Monthly Budgetary Report, 2008–2021)

processing firms. Table 4.1 provides a step-by-step overview of Palestinian traders' interactions in importing products into the West Bank or Gaza. As the table illustrates, the interaction between traders and the PA was superficial, with the Israeli private and public sectors processing and monitoring the entire transaction.

Second, the Israeli authorities and Israeli private sector benefited from these imports at various economic levels. Palestinian traders were forced to hire Israeli firms to represent them during the processing and clearance of shipments. Furthermore, Israeli bonded warehouses charged traders storage fees and costs while shipments were being processed (Elkhafif et al. 2014, p. 19; Iqtait 2021, p. 261). The World Bank estimated that the average duration for import processes in 2015 was 38 days, leading to significantly high storage costs (World Bank 2017, p. 44). Additionally, Palestinian traders were forced to hire Israeli firms to transport their imports from ports to the West Bank or Gaza Strip. In addition to the costs incurred at the individual level, Israeli authorities deducted three per cent of the total value of VAT and customs collected before crediting the PA's account.

The third effect of clearance revenue was that the mechanism's costly and complicated dealings and procedures incentivised Palestinian traders to rely on Israeli counterparts to complete the importation process.

84    A. IQTAIT

**Table 4.1** Palestinian traders' interaction with Israel and PA[3]

| Actions | Responsible Party |
| --- | --- |
| Palestinian traders issue Certificate of Importation from PA (only prerequisite for international imports) | PA |
| Shipment arrival to Israeli Port (Haifa or Ashdod) | Israel |
| Hire Israeli Clearance and Processing Agents | Israel |
| Administrative procedures: processing, valuation, and storage | Israel |
| Issuance of initial Custom and VAT Certificate | Israel |
| Settlement of Custom and VAT amount | Israel |
| Issuance of final Custom and VAT Certificate | Israel |
| Shipment transported, via Israeli trucks, to Israeli military crossing in West Bank or Gaza Strip | Israel |
| Shipment is unloaded from Israeli trucks, inspected, then loaded onto Palestinian trucks (back-to-back system) (occasional occurrence) | Israel |
| Shipment transported to Palestinian market, where additional Israeli checkpoints, and inspections may occur | Palestinian or Israeli private sector |
| Palestinian traders submit VAT and Custom certificates to PA | PA |

While this process took 38 days to complete for Palestinian traders, their Israeli counterparts completed the same procedures in ten days. Similarly, the average cost per transaction for Israeli traders was a third of the cost for their Palestinian counterparts in 2015, at USD 565 and USD 1425, respectively (World Bank 2017). As such, Palestinian businessmen imported products through Israeli intermediaries who, in turn, sold their imports to their Palestinian counterparts after the importation process had been completed. This diversion lowered the import processing time for Palestinian traders by 75 per cent and cut the cost of importation by 60 per cent.

Fourth, Palestinian traders importing products through Israeli intermediaries caused significant fiscal leakages for the PA under the clearance revenue mechanism. Customs and VAT were collected on international

---

[3] This table was constructed based on author interviews with Palestinian traders, PA officials, and Hanan Taha-Rayyan, Chief Executive Officer of Palestine Trade Centre, West Bank, 2017 and 2020.

imports that were destined for PA areas, but imports from Israel were only eligible for VAT according the custom union principles of the Paris Protocol (Article III). The World Bank reported similar findings.

> A large number of Palestinian businesses use Israeli middlemen to import goods from third countries because procedures are seen as simpler and less time consuming relative to those applied to direct imports. For example, Palestinian importers need to apply for an import license every time they import merchandise while Israeli importers are granted a one-year license. Palestinian businesses also report that regulations governing direct importing are revised often by the Israeli authorities and are only available in Hebrew which makes it difficult for Palestinian importers to meet them. As a result, indirect imports enter the Palestinian market as Israeli goods, which makes the Palestinian Authority only eligible for VAT collected on them according to the Paris Protocol. Other import duties collected on these goods are retained by the Government of Israel, resulting in a fiscal loss for the Palestinian Authority. (World Bank 2016, p. 14)

Fifth, in addition to Palestinian traders' use of Israeli intermediaries, the clearance revenue mechanism incentivised a wide range of tax evasion practices. These practices included under-reporting of VAT or customs paid to Israel, undervaluation, fraud, and smuggling, and an indirect importation through Israeli intermediaries (as described above). The total fiscal loss to the PA was estimated at 3.2 per cent of GDP annually, equalling about USD 5.6 billion between 2000 and 2017 (United Nations Conference on Trade and Development [UNCTAD] 2019, p. 17). Palestinian traders resorted to indirect importation due to the PA's lack of control over resources and weak domestic productive base, the long-established relationship between Palestinian and Israeli traders, customs limitations and high customs costs, and the high number of administrative obstacles set by Israel or the PA (Habbas 2021). Other factors that incentivised tax evasion through the clearance revenue mechanism included the PA's inability to establish a social contract based on taxation, as will be investigated in Chapter 5. As such, the economic consequences of the clearance revenue mechanism undermined the PA's ability to exert a monopoly over Palestinian fiscal revenues. This thwarted PA efforts to create a social contract with segments of Palestinian society. On the contrary, fiscal leakages resulting from the mechanism meant that Palestinian traders continued to pay taxes to the Israeli government in lieu of the PA.

## 4.5   PA Fiscal Policy: Rentier-Driven Expansion and Contraction Cycles

Although the PA did not possess the means of setting independent economic policies, it had evolved its fiscal anatomy to accommodate two levels of fiscal allocation cycles. These policies depended primarily on the amount of foreign aid disbursed by donors each year, the undisturbed transfer of clearance revenue by Israel, and the accumulation of arrears against the private sector.

The first level ensured the fiscal survival of the PA, represented by a fiscal allocation cycle that met its basic recurrent expenditures, which included its wage bill, social transfers, and operational expenditures. This policy relied on the PA's ability to secure clearance revenue from Israel on regular basis. In addition, it relied on a basic level of foreign aid disbursement by donors through the PA's budget. Although budgetary aid levels fluctuated, there was a certain threshold of guaranteed support from donors to the PA's budget. From 2007 onward, budgetary support did not fall below USD 500 million annually. Ali Jarbawi of Birzeit University, and former PA Minister of Development and Planning, noted: 'Donors will not reduce aid levels beyond a basic threshold which seems to have hovered around USD 500–700 million' (author interview with Ali Jarbawi, Birzeit, 2017).

Thus, with basic foreign aid levels and consistent clearance revenue transfers, the PA could sustain its fiscal position and meet its basic allocative obligations. However, under this cycle the PA accumulated significant arrears to the public sector pension fund, municipalities and private suppliers to finance its deficit. Arrears accumulation typically offset low budgetary support levels, and formed ten per cent of annual PA expenditures. In addition to arrears, the PA relied on loans from the banking sector. In 2020, the PA had a stock of total debt liabilities of about 47 per cent of GDP. Domestic debt stood at 39 per cent of GDP, with arrears to private suppliers and pension fund equalling 25 per cent of GDP and domestic bank loans equalling 14 per cent of GDP (IMF 2022, p. 34). Arrears to private suppliers exerted immense pressure on the wider Palestinian economy and undermined liquidity within the private sector (Iqtait 2021, p. 263). Chapter 5 will highlight how the PA politicised this component of the budget to coerce the business community in an attempt to enhance domestic tax mobilisation. Although PA loans from domestic banks equalled only 21 per cent of total loans, they represented 111 per cent of banks' total equity (IMF 2022, p. 11). In addition, loans to PA employees doubled banks' exposure to the public sector. Thus, under the first allocative fiscal cycle, the PA would meet its basic obligations while accumulating debt against different sectors of the economy.

The second level was an expansionary fiscal allocation cycle and was contingent on higher foreign aid disbursements through the PA's budget. The PA experienced two foreign aid expansionary cycles in recent years; these occurred between 2007 and 2010 and between 2013 and 2014, and financed around 51 per cent and 32 per cent of the PA's budget, respectively. In 2008, for example, donors funnelled 80 per cent of their aid disbursements through the PA's budget, which amounted to 60 per cent of the PA's total expenditures for that year (Chapter 3).[4] In addition to meeting its recurrent expenditures, during these cycles the PA expanded its development expenditures budget and reduced the accumulated arrears and loans.

During expansionary cycles the PA inflated its development budget, which, in turn, was donor-driven and consisted of fragmented development projects designed, funded, and often implemented by donors or under donors' supervision through the PA's budget (author interviews with Ali Jarbawi, Birzeit, 2017). Although many of these projects, such as the construction of schools and health clinics, were intended to expand the PA's service delivery capacity, they reflected the PA's inability to meet its own developmental expenditures. As Fadi Kattan notes, 'there was a correlation between the PA's development budget and the amount of foreign aid allocated to the PA's budget' (author interviews with Fadi Kattan, Ali Jarbawi). As such, the development budget was a function of the availability of foreign aid and the PA had little control over the timing or distribution of these funds. In addition, the expansion of the development budget did not necessarily translate to higher PA legitimacy because it was seen as weak and incapable of constructing services delivery infrastructure (author interviews with Khalil Shahin, Ramallah 2017, Fadi Kattan).

However, the PA's management of external income reflected its dynamic search for means to secure its fiscal continuity and mimic state responsibilities within a dual rentier framework. One such policy was the issuance of PA treasury bonds during contractionary cycles. Although the

---

[4] Ibid.

PA had instituted the Law of Public Debt in 2005, which enabled it to issue state debt, only in 2014 did the PA issue its first sale of government bonds (Wafa 2005; Browning 2014). The PA introduced these bonds to restructure debt to domestic banks with low-interest rates. PA bonds were encouraged and sponsored by donors. In 2014, the IMF praised 'the positive role that the issuance of government bonds could play for financial stability, and views securitisation of government debt as an important step in support of banks' liquidity management and, ultimately, towards developing a domestic debt market' (IMF 2014, p. 19).

In 2016, the PA started to issue promissory notes, or zero interest bonds, to the private sector as part of the arrears mechanism. While donors initially neglected this issue because they were focused on decreasing the PA's deficit, these bonds increased the PA's exposure to the private sector. PA bonds also made it easier for the government to receive services from private suppliers at a premium. Promissory note holders had the option to cash in their debt at a local bank in exchange for a discount cash payment of eight per cent (World Bank 2016). This transferred much of the arrears debt from Palestinian businesses to the banking sector. Most importantly, however, this meant that the PA was underpaying for services from the private sector; this agitated a large number of suppliers, who viewed this as 'predatory behaviour and further justification for tax evasion' (author interview with Chamber of Commerce and Industry in Ramallah and Al Bireh Governorate member, Ramallah, 2017 and 2020). This did not deter the PA from utilising its higher financial exposure to the private sector as a bargaining tool to request higher foreign aid transfers from donors (Iqtait 2021, 264). This tactic enjoyed a little success, but donors later realised the financial risks associated with this move: 'In light of the recent decline in external budget support, and with over two thirds of public revenues consisting of clearance revenues that are subject to unplanned disruptions, this is very risky', noted a report by the World Bank (2016, p. 7). The PA's fiscal expansionary and contractionary cycles were rentier-driven and affected its relationship with the wider economy through the arrears system and other debt accumulation, in addition to constructing services delivery infrastructure.

## 4.6 The PA's Rentier Trap

Israel's continued occupation, donors' influence over PA priorities and policies, the PA's fixation with securing clearance revenue and foreign aid, and the under-sized productive base in West Bank and Gaza perpetuated the PA's dependence on rentier income. This manifested in the macroeconomic structure in the form of rent-driven consumption and a rentier trap for the PA.

The following equation best captures available consumption in Palestine according to the National Accounts calculations of the PCBS:

$$C_{total} = \left(C_{household} + C_{governemnt} + C_{NPISH}\right)$$

The PCBS divided total consumption into household consumption, government consumption and Non-Profit Institutions Serving Households (NPISH) consumption (PCBS, n.d.). Each of these three components was induced by external income. Household consumption was fuelled by remittances from Palestinian labourers in Israel or other remittances from abroad; government consumption was induced by foreign aid and clearance revenue; and NPISH consumption was financed by foreign aid to Palestinian NGOs and other international organisations.

Total consumption is also a function of gross disposable income, which is total consumption and total savings in the economy. Palestine, like many external income-dependent developing countries, had a GNDI significantly larger than its domestic production, or economic output, indicating a much larger capacity to consume in comparison to available resources within the limits of the Palestinian economy. On average, GNDI value has been 29 per cent higher than GDP in Palestine since 1994. GNDI was allocated almost entirely for consumption with only three per cent being saved (PCBS, n.d.).

Figure 4.2 displays the PA's position within the wider macroeconomic structure. The PA was a major distributor of rents in the form of foreign aid and recycled rents in the form of clearance revenue. This translated to a rentier trap for the PA, whereby increasing total revenues was contingent on the increase in total external income available to the wider economy.

As Fig. 4.2 details, rentier income to the Palestinian economy accrued in the form of remittances and foreign aid. Remittances were expended on consumption. Foreign aid was disbursed through several channels and expended either through the PA's budget or through an array of domestic or international organisations (such as NGOs, USAID or UNRWA). Both

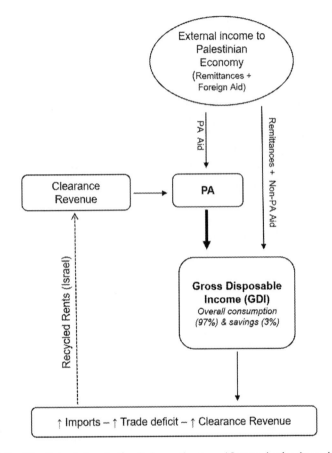

**Fig. 4.2** The Palestinian Authority's rentier trap (*Source* Author's analysis)

channels were expended in the domestic economy and funded overall consumption. Due to the economy's small domestic production base, domestic demand was met through higher rates of imports from Israel or the international markets, increasing the trade deficit. Imports amounted to 50 per cent of final consumption, while taxes on imports amounted to around 77 per cent of total tax revenues for the PA (PCBS, n.d.). Consequently, imports financed rent extraction by Israel in the form of customs, VAT, and fuel excises. The extracted rents were thereafter transferred to the PA through the clearance revenue mechanism. In order for the PA to increase its overall revenue, it had to increase its externally accrued revenue and the overall rents available to the wider economy. This raises the question of whether the PA designed or reinforced this structure, or whether it was an unintended consequence of the larger political situation. Eljafari argues that this structure was the result of a conscious decision by the PA in 'the absence of its ability to raise taxes domestically'. He adds:

> The PA's ministry of finance determinedly attempts to maximise its budgetary revenues regardless of other [economic] parameters. As a result expanding the trade deficit was favourably viewed and tolerated as long as clearance revenues managed to offset the costs of PA salaries. In a strange way, the ministry works against the healthiness of the Palestinian economy. (author interview with Mahmoud Eljafari, Ramallah, 2017)

Ali Jarbawi agrees:

> The PA [after all] is a rentier entity. Whether it is aid or other Israeli controlled revenues, the fixation within the PA will continue to be maximise revenues and distribute salaries. Even if this arrangement entails deepening an economic structure that is based on income from abroad or other forms of rents. (author interview with Ali Jarbawi, Birzeit, 2017)

## 4.7   Conclusion

As this chapter has demonstrated, many of the prevalent economic pathologies in the Palestinian economy—including a weak productive sector, excessive unemployment, high levels of local consumption, and a volatile macroeconomic environment—are embedded in an inherited economic structure characterised by an excessive reliance on external income in the form of foreign aid and remittances. Although this structure evolved under Israel's control between 1967 and 1993, the PA's attempts to reduce this dependence through its economic agreements with Israel, and particularly the Paris Protocol, were unsuccessful.

While the larger political environment of Israeli occupation was pertinent, the economic consequences of rent dependency could not have been averted. The structural composition of the Palestinian economy suffered, with the continuing erosion of the industrial and agricultural sectors. Foreign aid and remittances funded ballooning imports from Israel and the rest of the world. In addition, the cost of labour and capital was high relative to the per capita income, further disincentivising economic activity in productive sectors. Rents afforded Palestinians considerably higher living standards relative to available economic resources. As such, Dutch Disease symptoms accelerated and became entrenched after the creation of the PA. This chapter also detailed how the erosion of the productive capacity of the economy and the adoption of external income-driven development plans created a rentier paradox for the PA. While external income was necessary for economic growth given the current economic structure, it further eroded the economy's ability to generate growth independent of rentier income.

The PA's fixation on securing clearance revenue and attracting foreign aid undermined its domestic tax collection efforts. Deficient tax policies—in the form of weak governance procedures to collect and monitor tax collection mechanisms, and lack of political motivation by PA officials and Ministry of Finance and Planning staff to mobilise taxes domestically—further weakened the PA's ability to raise taxes. The clearance revenue mechanism sidelined the PA from the trade process with Israel and world markets, and resulted in significant fiscal leakages due to tax evasion, corruption and tax avoidance. These mechanisms fostered a divide between the PA and Palestinian society and reinforced pre-PA economic links between Palestinian and Israeli traders, as well as between Palestinian traders and the Israeli government.

Although the PA showed little active inclination to decrease external income dependency and rentierism, it did evolve several policies to manage the flow of foreign aid and clearance revenue and increase its bargaining position vis-à-vis donors and Israel. Fiscal expansionary and contractionary cycles, as well as drawing debt from the private sector through government bonds and promissory notes, coerced segments of society and entangled the wider economy in the fiscal viability of the PA. This was associated with the PA's failure to account to the public, taxpayers, or credit providers and agitated wide segments of society against the PA's mishandling of funds and underpayment for services. In addition, the PA, relative to the wider economy, resided within a multi-rentier structure that necessitated the continuation of rentier income for survival.

## REFERENCES

Ahern, Mark Eugene. 2017. *Economic Monitoring Report to the Ad Hoc Liaison Committee.* Washington, DC: World Bank.

Arnon, Arie, and Jimmy Weinblatt. 2001. 'Sovereignty and Economic Development: The Case of Israel and Palestine.' *The Economic Journal* 111, no. 472: F295–F298295.

Bank of Israel. 2010. *Recent Economic Developments, No. 128 (August).* https://www.boi.org.il/en/NewsAndPublications/PressReleases/Pages/101004d.aspx.

Barghouti, Omar. 2011. *Resistance as an Indispensable Component of Development under Colonial Conditions: Boycott Divestment and Sanctions as a Case Study.* Working Paper, Center for Development Studies, Birzeit University. https://core.ac.uk/download/pdf/86429588.pdf.

BBC. 2001. *Gaza's Shattered Dreams (17 November 2001).* http://news.bbc.co.uk/2/hi/programmes/from_our_own_correspondent/1660621.stm.

Bisan Center. 2011. *Wahm al-Tanmeya/The Myth of Development.* Ramallah: Bisan Center for Research and Development.

Browning, Noah. 2014. *Palestinian Authority to Issue Debut Government Bonds to Banks to Restructure Debt. Reuters.* https://uk.reuters.com/article/palestinian-bonds/palestinian-authority-to-issue-debut-government-bonds-to-banks-to-restructure-debt-idUKL6N0N02Y920140408.

Chatelus, Michel, and Yves Schemeil. 1984. 'Towards a New Political Economy of State Industrialization in the Arab Middle East', *International Journal of Middle East Studies*, 16, no. 2: 251–65.

Coalition for Transparency and Integrity. 2017. *A Summary of Working Papers on Tax Evasion.* Ramallah: AMAN.

Elkhafif, Mahmoud, Misyef Misyef, and Mutasim Elagraa. 2014. *Palestinian Fiscal Revenue Leakage to Israel Under the Paris Protocol on Economic Relations.* United Nations Conference on Trade and Development.

Eltalla, Hakeem, and Luc Hens. 2009. *The Impact of Trade Transaction Costs on Palestine.* International Trade and Finance Association 19th International Conference Working Papers.

Farsakh, Leila. 2002. 'Palestinian Labor Flows to the Israeli Economy: A Finished Story?' *Journal of Palestine Studies* 32, no. 1: 13–27.

Gaza–Jericho Agreement, Annex IV (29 April 1994) Protocol on Economic Relations between the Government of the State of Israel and the P.L.O., representing the Palestinian People.

Habbas, Walid. 2021. 'The West Bank-Israel Economic Integration: Palestinian Interaction with the Israeli Border and Permit Regimes.' In *Political Economy of Palestine*, 111–34. Cham: Palgrave Macmillan.

94    A. IQTAIT

Hanieh, Adam. 2016. 'Development as Struggle: Confronting the Reality of Power in Palestine.' *Journal of Palestine Studies* 45, no. 4: 35.

Hassan, Shamir. 2011. 'Oslo Accords: The Genesis and Consequences for Palestine.' *Social Scientist* 39, no. 7/8: 65–72.

Ibrahim, Nassar, and Pierre Beaudet. 2012. 'Effective Aid in the Occupied Palestinian Territories?' *Conflict, Security and Development* 12, no. 5: 481–500.

International Monetary Fund (IMF). 2014. *West Bank and Gaza: Report on Macroeconomic Developments and Outlook.* https://www.imf.org/en/Countries/ResRep/WBG/News-Archive.

International Monetary Fund (IMF). 2022. *Report to the Ad Hoc Liaison Committee (2 May 2022).* https://www.imf.org/en/Publications/CR/Issues/2022/05/02/West-Bank-and-Gaza-Report-to-the-AD-HOC-Liaison-Committee-517501.

Iqtait, Anas. 2019. 'The Political Economy of Taming the Palestinian Authority.' In *Palestine: Past and Present,* edited by Tristan Dunning, 145–75. Nova Publishing.

Iqtait, Anas. 2021. 'The Palestinian Authority Political Economy: The Architecture of Fiscal Control.' In *Political Economy of Palestine,* edited by Alaa Tartir et al., 249–270. Cham: Palgrave Macmillan.

Israeli Central Bureau of Statistics (ICBS). 1993. *National Accounts of Judea, Samaria and the Gaza Area 1968–1993.* Jerusalem: ICBS.

Kanafani, Numan. 2001. 'Trade—A Catalyst for Peace?', *The Economic Journal* 11, no. 1: 276–90.

Khalidi, Raja, and Sobhi Samour. 2011. 'Neoliberalism as Liberation: The Statehood Program and the Remaking of the Palestinian National Movement.' *Journal of Palestine Studies* 40, no. 2: 10.

Koldas, Umut. 2017. 'From Coercion to Consent? The Paris Protocol and Contours of Hegemonic Economic Communication between the Israeli and Palestinian Societies.' *International Journal of Economic Perspectives* 11, no. 1: 740–52.

Le More, Anne. 2010. *International Assistance to the Palestinians After Oslo: Political Guilt, Wasted Money.* New York, NY: Routledge.

Mansour, Antoine. 1988. 'The West Bank Economy: 1948–1984.' In *The Palestinian Economy,* edited by George Abed, 71–99. London: Routledge.

Palestine Economic Policy Research Institute. 2012. *Food Security Bulletin.* Palestine Economic Research Institute.

Palestinian Authority. 2005. 'Public Debt Law 24 (2005).' http://info.wafa.ps/ar_page.aspx?id=2621.

Palestinian Central Bureau of Statistics (PCBS). 2020. Registered Foreign Trade Statistics—Goods and Services, 2019: Main Results. Ramallah—Palestine. https://www.pcbs.gov.ps/Downloads/book2537.pdf

Palestinian Central Bureau of Statistics (PCBS). 2022. Palestinian Labour Force Survey Annual Report: 2021. Ramallah—Palestine. https://www.pcbs.gov. ps/Downloads/book2605.pdf.

Palestinian Central Bureau of Statistics (PCBS). n.d. 'National Accounts Variables in Palestine for the Years 1994–2020 at Current Prices.' http://www.pcbs. gov.ps/site/lang__en/741/default.aspx.

Palestinian Investment Promotion Agency. n.d. 'Tax.' http://www.pipa.ps/page. php?id=1bc27fy1819263Y1bc27f.

Petri, Peter. 1997. *Trade Strategies for The Southern Mediterranean*. OECD Development Centre Working Paper 127.

Ridao-Cano, Cristobal, Friederike Rother, and Javier Sanchez-Reaza. 2019. *West Bank and Gaza—Jobs in West Bank and Gaza Project: Enhancing Job Opportunities for Palestinians*. Washington, DC: World Bank. http://doc uments.worldbank.org/curated/en/523241562095688030/West-Bank-and-Gaza-Jobs-in-West-Bank-and-Gaza-Project-Enhancing-Job-Opportunities-for-Palestinians, accessed June 2019.

Roy, Sara. 1999. 'De-development Revisited: Palestinian Economy and Society since Oslo.' *Journal of Palestine Studies* 28, no. 3: 67–68.

Roy, Sara. 2007. *Failing Peace: Gaza and the Palestinian–Israeli Conflict*. London: Pluto Press.

Samhouri, Mohammed. 2016. 'Revisiting the Paris Protocol: Israeli–Palestinian Economic Relations, 1994–2014.' *The Middle East Journal* 70, no. 4: 579–607.

Shikaki, Ibrahim. 2021. 'The Political Economy of Dependency and Class Formation in the Occupied Palestinian Territories Since 1967.' In *Political Economy of Palestine*, 49–80. Cham: Palgrave Macmillan.

Tartir, Alaa, and Jeremy Wildeman. 2012. 'Persistent Failure: World Bank Policies for the Occupied Palestinian Territories.' *Al-Shabakka* (October).

Terme, Rosa Alonso, and Fadi Kattan. 2010. 'Mercantilism or Liberalism? Economic Autonomy and State-Building in Palestine.' In *The Palestinian Economy: Theoretical and Practical Challenges*, edited by Gianni Vaggi, Marco Missaglia, and Fadi Kattan, 40–43. Pavia: Pavia University Press.

The New York Times. 1988. 'Gaza City-State Could Be Singapore of Mideast (7 January 1988).' https://www.nytimes.com/1988/01/07/opi nion/l-gaza-city-state-could-be-singapore-of-mideast-365688.html.

United Nations Conference on Trade and Development. 2019. *Economic Costs of the Israeli Occupation for the Palestinian People: Fiscal Aspects*. https://unc tad.org/system/files/official-document/a74d272_en.pdf.

United Nations Office for the Coordination of Humanitarian Affairs (OCHA). 2012. *Fragmented Lives: Humanitarian Overview*. United Nations.

Wafa. 2005. *Palestinian Authority, Public Debt Law 24 (2005)*. http://info.wafa. ps/ar_page.aspx?id=2621.

96    A. IQTAIT

World Bank. 1993. *Developing the Occupied Territories: An Investment in Peace.*
World Bank. 2016. *Economic Monitoring Report to the Ad Hoc Liaison Committee
(19 April 2016).* http://documents.worldbank.org/curated/en/780371468
179658043/main-report.
World Bank. 2017. *Unlocking the Trade Potential of the Palestinian Economy.*
https://documents.worldbank.org/en/publication/documents-reports/doc
umentdetail/960071513228856631/unlocking-the-trade-potential-of-the-
palestinian-economy-immediate-measures-and-a-long-term-vision-to-improve-
palestinian-trade-and-economic-outcomes.

CHAPTER 5

# The Societal Legacy of Dual Rentierism

**Abstract** This chapter mobilises three influential representatives of Palestinian society—the Palestinian NGO sector, the PA's public servants, and the business community—to draw conclusions on how the Palestinian Authority's dual rentierism hindered its ability to instil a social contract with its society. The relationship between the international community and the PA, on the one hand, and between the PA and Israeli clearance revenue on the other, hindered the formation of a stable societal contract between the PA and different segments of Palestinian society. The chapter's primary argument is that the PA's commitments to abide by externally imposed conditionalities undermined its inward accountability and hindered its legitimacy. It further shifted the PA's accountability in favour of rent providers. The resultant state–society relationship was weak, and plagued by authoritarianism, lack of political institutions, mistrust, and competition. The evolution of a social contract based on taxation and representation was further undermined by the PA's weak domestic legitimacy.

**Keywords** Non-governmental organisations · Rentier bargain · Labour Unions · Private sector · Social contract · Conditionality

© The Author(s), under exclusive license to Springer Nature Switzerland AG 2023
A. Iqtait, *Funding and the Quest for Sovereignty in Palestine*,
https://doi.org/10.1007/978-3-031-19478-8_5

98    A. IQTAIT

# 5.1    Introduction

Little attention has been paid to the effects of foreign aid and clearance revenue on the PA–society relationship. This chapter seeks to address this gap, drawing on in-depth interviews conducted primarily in the West Bank in 2017 and 2020. Chapter 1 addressed the concepts of the state and the PA, noting that while the PA was not a state, it will be treated as one for the purpose of analysis in this book. That applies equally to this chapter. In treating the PA as a state, this chapter is not attempting to trivialise the pervasive role of the Israeli occupation in shaping social relations in Palestine.[1] Rather, this chapter explores PA–society relations and how foreign aid and clearance revenue affected those relations since 1994.

The chapter opens up for analysis foreign aid and clearance revenue delivery mechanisms whereby Israel and donors distributed rents through the PA or other segments of Palestinian society. The resulting dynamic was that a substantial portion of rents was channelled beyond the PA's control, which provided leverage for different actors and forces in the political economy and directly influenced the PA's ability to actively co-opt or coerce its society. The role rent providers play in shaping relations between the state and its society through different types of condition-alities is also explored. Donors' conditions for disbursing foreign aid ranged from total transparency to active engagement in the PA's societal engagement. Procedural conditionality imposed by Israel on transferral of clearance revenue played an instrumental role in shaping the PA's relationship with the Palestinian business community.

The PA itself was inconsistent in its attempts to set the terms of its relationship with Palestinian society. It pursued, at times, conflicting poli-cies to co-opt different societal segments, or demanded varying levels of acquiescence depending on historical or political considerations.

The chapter investigates the preceding relations by analysing the PA's interaction with three important segments of its society: the NGO sector; the PA's own public sector, with an emphasis on the role of public teachers; and the private sector, represented by several segments of the business community. The three segments are situated differently relative to the PA's rentier trap (introduced in Chapter 4). The NGO sector was

---

[1] For a discussion of Israel's impact on Palestinian society see, for example, Roy (2001), Muslih (1993), Ophir et al. (2009), and Hilal (2002) [in Arabic].

a direct competitor for foreign aid disbursements. The PA's public sector was the main beneficiary of its rentier structure, with at least 50 per cent of all PA expenditure servicing its wage bill. Finally, the business community's import activity with or through Israel generated the main source of clearance revenue. Each case presented challenges to the PA's ambitions to instil a rentier bargain over Palestinian society, and demonstrates the PA's diverse tactics of co-optation—primarily driven by its dual rentierism.

## 5.2 Foreign Aid and Non-Governmental Organisations Pre-1994

Palestinian NGOs started largely as welfare organisations in the 1930s and 1940s and evolved to a full 'third sector' (as contrasted with the governmental and private sectors) after the Israeli occupation of the West Bank and Gaza in 1967 (Sullivan 1996, p. 94). The 1970s and 1980s saw a significant proliferation in the number of Palestinian NGOs. During this period, many NGOs operated independently of existing Israeli service-provision systems in the West Bank and Gaza but were placed under heavy restrictions for the establishment or registration of new organisations (Jarrar 2005). The expansion of the NGO sector was despite—indeed, because of—the Israeli occupation. NGOs in sovereign states mediate and bridge relations between society and the state, and, at times, provide services to marginalised or under-represented segments of society. By definition, NGOs operate under the umbrella of a national central authority (Challand 2009). In Palestine, however, NGOs emerged as an alternative to the state, to compensate for the absence of a government capable of providing basic services (Al-Barghouthi 2009). In addition to providing services, NGOs held a more traditional role as society agents capable of grassroots mobilisation for political and social causes. For example, NGOs played a pivotal role in the early years of the 1987 Intifada by fostering poverty alleviation programs, public awareness movements, and civil disobedience campaigns, and by representing marginalised communities (Ayed 1998; Labib 1992, p. 360).

After 1991, NGOs underwent a transformation, in part as a consequence of domestic and international events. NGOs had traditionally received funding from a multitude of Palestinian, Arab, and international actors. However, funding from the PLO, Arab regional actors and Soviet-backed social movements had subsided by the end of the 1980s. In addition, Islamic society and political organisations (such as

Hamas) gradually took over the roles of grassroot service delivery and social and political mobilisation (see Roy 2011; Taraki 1989, pp. 30–32; Baconi 2018). Nonetheless, the most important factor in this transition was NGOs' evolution into professional rent-seekers in the global aid industry (author interview with Izzat Abdulhadi, Canberra, 2018). By 1993, the most influential NGOs in the West Bank and Gaza had evolved into professional, development-oriented, and foreign-funded organisations (Hammami 2000, p. 17). NGOs prioritised the securitisation of foreign aid, which by this stage became almost exclusively concentrated in the Western block. When the PA was established in 1993, there were approximately 1500 operating NGOs employing up to 30,000 persons and receiving more than USD 220 million per year in external funding operating in the West Bank and Gaza (Brynen 2000, pp. 49–50).

Foreign funding, however, implied a set of new conditionalities, as donors were interested in the professionalisation and de-politicisation of the sector. Professionalisation meant maximising the efficiency of the services provision apparatuses directed by NGOs in the West Bank and Gaza. It also entailed developing new planning, reporting, and monitoring skills to satisfy foreign donors' requirements and project management standards. Consequently, by 1994 many NGOs had integrated into the global aid industry, and successfully developed the language, culture, and methodologies necessary for securing donor funding (Brynen 2000, pp. 49–50). NGOs' transformation also entailed complying with rigid political conditionalities that ensured the de-politicisation of the sector. Previously, NGOs secured funding from Palestinian individuals and factions, or political sympathisers of the Palestinian national movement, and were charged with political goals (author interviews with Izzat Abdulhadi, Canberra, 2018, and Dua'a Qurie, Ramallah, 2017). However, international donors were clear in their focus on the humanitarian needs and living conditions of the Palestinians, and tried to avoid political dimensions. As a consequence, NGOs turned mostly to services delivery and research or development centres concerned with improving the living standards of Palestinians or monitoring and reporting the economic or humanitarian conditions in the West Bank and Gaza (author interview with Izzat Abdulhadi).

### 5.2.1 Competition Over Foreign Aid: Mistrust and Legitimacy

Donors recognised the entrenchment of NGOs in Palestine and acknowledged their role as an important pillar in servicing the peace process objectives and aiding the PA in its negotiations with Israel (author interview with UN official, Ramallah, 2017). This recognition translated directly to significant financial support. For example, the World Bank's technical report on the creation and financing of the PA, published in 1994, showcased that 52 per cent of all foreign aid destined to 'Central Administration start-up expenditures' was dedicated to the NGO sector (World Bank 1994, p. 14). As the World Bank explained:

> During the past 25 years, Palestinian society has developed a spectrum of institutions and organizations which supplement the services provided by the public sector and which are an important part of the social safety net of the occupied territory ... Given its important role, the NGO sector is an immensely valuable resource, particularly during the transitional period while new institutions are still being developed. The program would provide support for essential activities of NGOs (in education, health and agriculture), and for general welfare activities, under conditions that enforce accountability, transparency and minimum professional standards. (1994, pp. 14–15)

The trust and support of the World Bank translated to USD 117 million in funding between 1994 and 1996 alone. In comparison, the PA received USD 108 million during the same period for the same purpose, the Central Administration start-up expenditures (World Bank 1994).

With external funding, the NGO sector emerged as an important actor in the evolving political economy space following the Oslo Accords. The sector's relationship with the PA revolved around legal issues pertaining to PA's regulation of the sector and NGOs' participation in formulating public policies. As Naseer Aruri (1994, p. 17) explains, NGOs at this juncture feared that PA governance would impose high levels of control over the sector, similar to those existing in neighbouring Arab states. As expected, the PA attempted to control the sector and called on all NGOs operating in the West Bank and Gaza to register for licensing by 1994 (Brynen 1996, p. 85). NGOs not only refused to comply with the PA's requests, citing concerns over censorship but also proposed several laws and drafted policy papers on the right of NGOs to operate freely

102     A. IQTAIT

and receive foreign funding independent of PA oversight (Sullivan 1996; author interview with Izzat Abdulhadi).

Monitoring tensions between the PA and NGOs closely, the World Bank announced in 1995 an initiative to create a USD 15 million NGO Trust Fund in the West Bank and Gaza.[2] The PA was not enthusiastic about the proposal, preferring funds to flow directly through its budget (Brynen 1996, p. 86). As Hammami (2000, p. 17) describes, this call aggravated tensions between the PA and NGOs and marked a shift in PA's perception of the sector, from being a 'mere political irritation' to becoming an 'actual political threat'. A primary concern of the PA was the ability of NGOs to attract and secure large sums of foreign aid from international actors and, consequently, to challenge the PA's financial hegemony. In response, the PA issued a series of official and unofficial policies designed to coerce or marginalise the NGO sector. Such attempts included the PA's successful ratification of the 'Charitable Associations and Community Organisations Law', which required NGOs to register with the Ministry of Interior and to provide full regular disclosure of operations, financing and activities.[3] Although many observers considered the law very liberal within the regional context, the PA's veto power over NGO creation and control over funding was strongly criticised.[4] Moreover, the PA created a Ministry of NGOs Affairs to regulate the relationship between international donors, international NGOs and local NGOs (Schwartz 2004; Hanafi and Tabar 2003, p. 209). The Ministry was short-lived, however, as it could not fulfil its duties in face of local and international objections (author interview with Dua'a Qurie, Ramallah, 2017).

Tensions between the PA and the NGO sector peaked following the publication of a United Nations report in 1999 on the development of the rule of law (Office of the Special Coordinator in the Occupied Territories 1999). The report stated that USD 100 million in aid was spent in Palestine between 1994 and 1999 to enhance the rule of law. The PA accused the NGO sector of gobbling most of the funds, citing mishandling, corruption, and allegations of implementing an external agenda

---

[2] The Fund initiative was proposed in 1995 and only became operational in 1998; see World Bank (1997).

[3] Palestinian Legislative Council, Law of Charitable Associations and Community Organisations (Law No. 1, Year 2000) January 2000.

[4] For a summary of the law see Jamal (2001, pp. 8–9) and Challand (2009, pp. 62–66).

(Challand 2009, pp. 65–66; Hammami et al. 2001). The PA's Ministry of Justice, in particular, ran a large media campaign to discredit the NGO sector as foreign agents. To counter the PA's crackdown, the NGO sector unified under several umbrellas, the most notable of which was the Palestinian Non-Governmental Organisations Network (PNGO), a coalition of 62 influential and well-financed NGOs (author interview with Dua'a Qurie). The PNGO further secured a coalition with the powerful Union of Charitable Associations, adding another 300 organisations to its representation (Jarrar 2005). During this process, the PA tried to fund and empower loyal NGOs to compete for donor funding, but this attempt failed as the professionalisation and de-politicisation of non-PA NGOs were more appealing to donors (author interview with Dua'a Qurie).

As such, throughout the early years of the PA, the donors played a paradoxical role. They injected billions in foreign aid and start-up capital to the PA, and simultaneously funded the NGO sector to undertake similar activities. The World Bank viewed the NGO sector as a necessary 'mechanism for service delivery' in the 'deteriorating socio-economic situation for Palestinians in the West Bank and Gaza coupled with the Palestinian Authority's unwillingness or inability to take on most social service delivery' (Sullivan 2001, p. 5). Donors treated the sector as a substitute for the PA, with a complementary role in professional and apolitical services delivery. In addition to funding, donors exerted political influence and often lobbied on behalf of the NGO sector. According to Curmi and Sullivan, the World Bank's support of Palestinian NGOs in general, and the PNGO network in particular, was the first time the World Bank directly financed NGOs without any state intervention (Sullivan 2001; Curmi 2002). Dua'a Qurie, the head of the PNGO Network commented: 'Donors were supportive of a strong NGO sector in the early years of the PA. [The] World Bank was responsive to the sector's demands and concerns about the PA or its attempts to rule over the sector. Frequently, the Bank would indirectly side with large NGOs through publishing technical reports or announce NGO-only funding schemes' (author interview with Dua'a Qurie).

Although the PA and NGO sector rivalry revolved around several themes, the inner political dynamics of this competition were fuelled by the availability of foreign aid funding to the NGO sector. Therefore, centralising all donor funding was at the forefront of the PA's confrontation with the sector, and the PA requested all foreign aid be channelled through the PA's controlled Palestinian Economic Council for Development and Reconstruction (PECDAR) or the Ministry of Planning and International Cooperation (Curmi 2002, pp. 113–16). For the PA, centralising foreign aid would have ensured hegemony over the NGO sector and provided a sense of legitimacy. The PA's objectives were not to contest the underlying objectives of donors' programs but, rather, to secure the funds associated with these programs (author interview with Khalil Shikaki, Ramallah, 2017). In the process, the PA would extend its hegemony over an influential component of Palestinian society.

Following the Oslo process years and the Palestinian Intifada of 2000–2005, the NGOs drastically changed their goals, structures, and composition. This transformation has been the subject of study by numerous researchers and analysts regarding the effect of NGO and donor funding on wider Palestinian society. The missing link within these studies, however, has been the NGO sector's embryonic relationship with the PA. As demonstrated above, during the early years of the PA this relationship was characterised by competition over foreign funding. But after 2007, the PA expanded its fiscal capacity and managed to attract greater sums of foreign aid from donors. Post-2007 relationships between the PA and the NGO sector can be divided into two distinct periods. The first was during the tenure of Salam Fayyad, who served as prime minister between 2007 and 2013; and the second was the post-Fayyad era.

Fayyad, a former IMF and World Bank economist, first entered the PA when former Palestinian President Yasser Arafat appointed him as finance minister in 2002. Fayyad, an international community favourite for his political independence, demanded autonomy to restructure Palestinian financial records and integrity. Fayyad presented an alternative to the shadowy administrative practices rampant during the early years of the PA. During his first year as finance minister, Fayyad disclosed the diversion of USD 900 million by the PA to personal accounts (Bennett and Nashashibi 2003). He started to centralise financial public records, convinced Arafat to disclose secretive personal accounts of the PA, and spearheaded the financial and fiscal reformation of the PA. Following the 2007 factional division between Fatah and Hamas, and the consequent geographical, administrative and political split between the West Bank and Gaza, Fayyad was appointed as both prime minister and finance minister of the PA. Fayyad's appointment was received favourably by the international community, which pledged USD 7.4 billion in aid to Palestinians between 2008 and 2011 (Murphy and Mohammed 2007). With international financial support, Fayyad launched his government's program: 'Palestine – Ending the Occupation, Establishing the State' (Palestine National Authority 2009).

Fayyad's plans caught the NGO community by surprise. NGOs, having lost significant societal support due to the professionalisation and de-politicisation processes they undertook during the early years of the PA, became 'attaché' agents for the international community to complement Fayyad's programs. In contrast to the earlier days of the PA, Fayyad did not view the NGO sector with hostility (author interview with Majdi Abu Zaid, Ramallah, 2017). He understood its ability to entice and secure vast sums of foreign aid. While Fayyad attracted more than USD 9.4 billion in international aid to the PA as direct budgetary support and development expenditure between 2007 and 2013, the NGO sector managed to secure nearly USD 3 billion during the same period (author interview with Dua'a Qurie). Nonetheless, the desire for financial hegemony was no longer a valid characterisation of the PA's position on NGOs. This was primarily due to the dual rentier structure of the PA. Fayyad's efficient transformation of the finance ministry and tax collection capacity translated to significant increases in the PA's net revenues. Non-aid PA revenue increased by 100 per cent between 2007 and 2013, granting the PA substantial fiscal freedom and leverage over the NGO sector (Iqtait 2020, p. 163). The PA's increased efficiency at domestic tax collection was accompanied by increased levels of clearance revenue recovery rates from Israel. The PA's increased fiscal coordination with Israel granted it pseudo-fiscal sovereignty based on consistent clearance revenue transfers and economic cooperation (Iqtait 2019; Dana 2015). Thus, the PA's fiscal and political leverage grew substantially under Fayyad compared to the NGO sector, which remained dependent solely on foreign aid.

Fayyad's institution-building programs not only maximised the amounts of foreign aid and clearance revenue granted to the PA, but also structurally transformed the priorities and objectives of donors. Previously, the World Bank and other donors had formulated, designed, and executed aid projects in the West Bank and Gaza independently of the PA. They also intentionally bypassed the PA regularly in favour of the NGO sector. However, under Fayyad, the World Bank, other donors and Israel facilitated the PA's agenda. Indeed, this facilitation was fundamentally associated with the fact that the PA was implementing plans that were aligned with Israel's security and further integrated the Palestinian and

Israeli economies (Iqtait 2021). The comprehensive vision of Fayyad's programs was to drive development through the PA as the central bureaucracy (author interview with Ali Jarbawi, Birzeit, 2017). Fayyad's drive for centralisation coincided with international efforts to restructure aid delivery mechanisms at a global scale, such as the Paris Declaration on Aid Effectives (2005) and the Accra Agenda for Action (2008). Both mechanisms emphasised the importance for developing countries of setting their own development strategies, and of donor countries aligning with these objectives and using the local systems proposed by the central bureaucracy in developing countries to achieve set strategies (OECD 2008). Accordingly, the PA both endorsed aid effectiveness mechanisms and formulated developmental models that adhered to their empirical and political objectives (author interview with Ali Jarbawi). Thus, the international community utilised the NGO sector during Fayyad's tenure not to bypass the PA but to strategically complement the PA's development efforts (author interview with Dua'a Qurie).

The NGO sector adapted to this change in policy in two ways. First, the vast majority of NGOs joined the PA's agenda and competed for generous foreign aid for short-term projects. An example of this approach was narrated by the director of a Ramallah-based NGO that received USD 34 million in donor funding between 2007 and 2013.

> There was a general sense of euphoria among the NGO sector during the early years of Fayyad's plans. Donors' focus was shifting from humanitarian relief work and temporary economic aid to marginalised families, towards capacity building in association with the PA. For the first time, we started to see independent NGOs partnering with PA ministries for project implementation. Donors encouraged these projects and favoured their organisers when reviewing funding proposals. (Author interview with Mohammad Salem, Ramallah, 2017)

Qurie also recalled: 'The quickest way to secure foreign funding during Salam Fayyad's tenure was to partner with any of the PA's ministries. Donors were constantly checking how their funds were going to contribute to the PAs institutional building efforts' (author interview with Dua'a Qurie).

Second, a small but influential group of NGOs resisted joining the PA's plans and innovated new strategies to secure foreign aid that centralised around two distinct themes. The first focused on promoting human rights, diversity, and tolerance. In an effort to remain independent of the PA, some NGOs appealed to donors for funding projects that observed the PA's evolving relationship with society, treated social injustices, and monitored the PA's security sector. However, donors only funded NGOs if their work focused exclusively on human rights and social injustice issues within Palestinian society, not as part of the wider context of Israeli occupation and the resultant human rights violations (author interview with Dua'a Qurie). As such, donors imposed strict conditionalities on the political and social dimensions of all donor-funded projects. Projects were expected to be apolitical towards Israel, renounce resistance against the Israeli occupation and avoid high-tension issues or themes, such as how Israeli settlements affected farmers. Many donors introduced extreme vetting processes and audits for all individuals and entities involved in any donor-funded activity. For example, in October 2007 the United States Agency for International Development (USAID) disseminated new rules and regulations for funding NGOs in Palestine. Qurie described the new rules as 'exclusionary, lack[ing] context, and pro-Israeli' (author interview with Dua'a Qurie). The USAID document, titled *Updated Anti-Terrorism Procedures, Update to Mission Order #21* (2007) provided expansive definitions of 'anti-terror funding' within the Palestinian setting (USAID 2007). On many occasions, having been arrested by the Israeli military provided sufficient grounds for USAID to reject funding proposals. This policy was particularly problematic because it excluded a large percentage of the Palestinian population. According to the Palestinian Central Bureau of Statistics, there have been one million detentions of Palestinians by the Israeli military since 1948 (PCBS 2017).

The second theme, initiated by a small number of NGOs who resisted joining the PA's programs, was reforming and monitoring the expanding NGO sector. The number of NGOs operating in Palestine had historically been high, but post-2007 hundreds of new, short-lived project-oriented NGOs emerged. Their numbers were estimated at 1230 in 2004 but reached at least 2400 in 2010 (Gerster 2013). The PA's laws on the creation and monitoring of NGOs—represented primarily by the aforementioned Charitable Associations and Community Organisations Law of 2000—were often bypassed. The availability of large sums of aid prompted a new class of specialised proposal writers and project managers, who were fluent in the conditionalities and thematic interests of international donors and purposefully drove their organisations' missions in alignment with those of international donors. As Merz (2012, p. 59),

Challand (2009) and Atia and Herrold (2018) argue, the donors' agenda 'and not the actual needs of the respective community' shaped many NGOs' missions and projects in Palestine.

The rapid increase in the number of NGOs unreservedly adopting donors' conditionalities impelled several well-established NGOs to lead a process of monitoring and regulating the NGO sector. However, the resultant attempt was entirely paradoxical, as the NGOs leading the monitoring and regulation process received technical analysis and funding from donors. Thus, donors' political conditionalities were imposed on the evolving NGO sector and on the NGOs attempting to regulate it. For example, the NGO Development Center (NDC), a leading Palestinian NGO based in Ramallah, designed a centralised digital portal and code of conduct for the Palestinian NGO sector. More than 1500 Palestinian NGOs had joined the portal and adhered to its code of conduct as of 2020 (NGO Development Center 2020). The Palestinian NGOs' code of conduct states:

> The signatories of this Document ... abide by the right to reject funding with politically-conditioned strings, since that is bound to distort the development process and/or undermine the legitimate struggle for independence and self-determination according to UN principles. The signatory NGOs also undertake to be in line with the national agenda without any normalization activities with the occupier, neither at the political-security nor the cultural or developmental levels. (NGO Development Center 2015)

However, the process of creating the code of conduct was advised by the World Bank and financed by the World Bank, the French Agency for Development, the European Union, the Islamic Development Bank and a donor consortium representing Switzerland, Denmark, the Netherlands and Sweden (NGO Development Center 2015). When members associated with the NDC were interviewed for the purposes of this research about the motives for launching the centralised portal and drafting the code of conduct, their answer was mainly to 'align NGO's priorities with those of the local communities'. But when asked about whether seeking funding from the very organisations that regularly imposed conditionalities on local NGOs was counterintuitive given the publicised goals of the code of conduct, they stressed that 'foreign funding was the only available option' for financing any NGO project (author interview with CEO of Ramallah-based NGO, Ramallah, 2017).

Against this backdrop, the NGO sector evolved in the Fayyad era into two groups of NGOs: those that complemented the PA's vision of institution-building, and those that decided to strategically carve new paths for appealing to donors by monitoring the PA or the NGO sector. However, all NGOs remained dependent on foreign funding, receiving billions in funding during the Fayyad era between 2007 and 2013. Consequently, the NGO sector became an essential employer in the Palestinian economy, accounting for more than 10 per cent of job opportunities in the Palestinian labour market (Gerster 2013, p. 23). Fayyad treated the NGO sector with flexibility. He supported the role it played in the implementation of his development strategy, as NGOs were involved in a variety of fields such as capacity-building, infrastructure development, services delivery, and women's empowerment programs. His government rarely fully enforced the Charitable Associations and Community Organisations Law, providing elastic legal boundaries for the formation and funding of NGOs (author interview with Majdi Abu Zaid). Fayyad's engagement with the sector stretched beyond formalities to include proactive involvement. Fayyad was the only Palestinian prime minister to frequently attend NGO-sponsored conferences, particularly those concerning the monitoring of the PA's financial and human right records. For example, Fayyad, as prime minister, attended all annual conferences of the Coalition for Accountability and Integrity (AMAN).[5] Despite AMAN's harsh assessment of the PA's corruption and transparency records, Fayyad frequently visited the centre and engaged with its reporting and methodologies (author interview with Majdi Abu Zaid).

It is essential to distinguish between Fayyad's approach to NGOs and the PA's general attitude towards the sector, however. PA officials, represented by Abbas and his inner circle, continued to consider the expanding NGO sector a political and fiscal threat (author interview with Khalil Shikaki). More specifically, PA officials viewed NGOs operating in human rights and monitoring fields as over-funded and controlled by donors' priorities (Hanafi and Tabar 2003, p. 209; author interviews

---

[5] AMAN is a leading corruption and governance transparency watchdog linked to Transparency International based in Ramallah; for more see https://www.aman-palestine.org/en.

with several PA officials, Ramallah, 2020). Many viewed Fayyad's policies towards NGOs as anti-Palestinian, citing the expansive influence and control foreign donors enjoyed over the sector. In 2010, Fayyad sought to transfer the power of regulating the NGO sector from the Ministry of Interior, as stipulated in the aforementioned 2000 law, to the Ministry of National Economy (Author interview with Majdi Abu Zaid). Although heavily criticised by NGOs and international donors for introducing firmer oversight over flows of foreign aid, the decision was an attempt by Fayyad to move the process of regulating the NGO sector in Palestine from the security to the civil sphere. Even after this decision, the enforcement of new laws and regulations remained lax despite considerable pressure from Abbas and his inner circle. Fayyad's successors, Rami Hamdallah and Mohammad Shtayyeh, have been more receptive to Abbas's demands and issued strict regulations requiring all NGOs to register for prior approval to receive local or international donations (Author interviews, West Bank, 2020). However, the implementation of these measures remained contested as donors and NGOs resisted these demands (author interviews with UN official, Ramallah, 2017, and Majdi Abu Zaid).

The PA's relationship with the NGO sector has evolved significantly since 1994. NGOs were first considered as an existential threat to the newly formed PA in the 1990s. The sector had considerable influence and received political and financial backing in its competition for recognition and involvement in the decision-making and policy drafting processes during the early years of the PA. Consequently, Fayyad considered the sector an integral part of Palestinian socioeconomic development and sought to utilise it to achieve his institution-building goals. The international community complied as it shifted its focus from utilising the sector often against the PA, towards strengthening the PA's centralised governance institutions and efficacy. It is clear that rents played an instrumental role in influencing the evolving relationship between the PA and NGO sector. International aid, through its multi-disbursement mechanisms via the PA and NGOs, meant that donors influenced the planning and implementation of their agendas. Furthermore, Fayyad's success in strengthening the PA's ability to secure a constant flow of clearance revenue granted it autonomy and fiscal independence. The double-rentier structure of the PA played a crucial role in shaping its relationship with the NGO sector. First, the PA's failure to centralise foreign aid disbursements away from NGOs weakened its ability to co-opt or coerce the NGO sector. Second, the PA's fixation with securing foreign aid and controlling the NGO sector resulted in mistrust and competition. Third, the PA's ability to exert hegemony over the sector, albeit partial, was due to donors' shifting preferences rather than an extension of local legitimacy. This further exacerbated the PA's domestic legitimacy, as it was viewed by the influential NGO sector as exogenous at worse and weak at best (author interviews with Dua'a Qurie, Khalil Shikaki, Majdi Abu Zaid, Ghada alMadbouh, and Jaad Issac, West Bank 2017).

## 5.3 Importing and Making a Rentier Class: The PA's Public Sector

The PA's dual rentier structure played a crucial role in sustaining the influence and control over another important actor in the Palestinian political economy: the public service. When the PA gradually assumed responsibility in the West Bank and Gaza after 1994, it faced labour market shocks leading to sudden and rapid increases in unemployment rates. The labour force at the time accounted for only a small share of total population, at only 19 per cent, and was composed primarily of private employment (74 per cent) and employment in Israel (18 per cent). Public sector employment formed less than eight per cent of total labour force participation. Only 20,000 people were employed by the public sector, and most of these were public school teachers or health workers (ICBS 1996).

The following years witnessed a rapid expansion in the number and function of public servants (Pannier 1996). The PA was undergoing a process of nation-building and creating a bureaucracy capable of sustaining state-like responsibilities. The process required a bureaucratic class capable of running day-to-day operations. While the international community provided the procedural blueprints and capital for the institutional build-up of the Palestinian central government, the recruitment and fulfilment of the public workforce was the responsibility of the PA. Thus, the PA began to build-up its workforce, hiring more than 32,000 additional people in its first three years of operations. By 1999, the PA boasted a workforce of 100,000 workers, which accounted for 20 per cent of total employment. The PA's increase in employment continued after its early years of operation and by 2020 reached more than 200,000 employees, representing 22 per cent of all employed individuals, as illustrated in Fig. 5.1 (PCBS 2022).

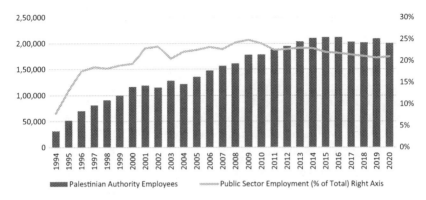

**Fig. 5.1** PA employees and public sector as percentage of total labour force, 1994–2020 (*Source* Calculated from Palestinian Central Bureau of Statistics data)

Two factors contributed to the growth in the number of public servants. The first was a by-product of the larger Palestinian political context represented by Israel's control over movement and access to the West Bank and Gaza. After 1993, Israeli authorities developed a rigid internal and external control system, severely restricting the flow of labour and products within the West Bank and Gaza or to Israel and the outside world (Bulmer 2003; Angrist 1996; Farsakh 2002). Restrictions on mobility led to a sharp decline in the number of Palestinians employed in the Israeli economy, driving an increase in the supply of labour to Palestinian markets. Restrictions also caused a decline in domestic economic activity, which in turn resulted in a decrease in demand for labour. Subsequently, the unemployment rate climbed to levels unforeseen in Palestine prior to 1993. Unemployment rates had skyrocketed to 15 per cent in 1998 and stayed consistently around 25 per cent from 2002. This exerted immense pressure on the PA to provide alternatives in a context where it lacked territorial or political control. The only way to generate employment, therefore, was for the PA to absorb a large number of unemployed individuals into its bureaucratic cadre and, as a result, increase public employment's share of total employment from eight per cent in 1994 to 22 per cent by 2020.

The second factor contributing to the growth of the public sector was related to the PA's political spheres of influence and control. At the core of these spheres was the PA's search for political legitimacy through co-optation and bureaucratic inclusion (author interview with Ali Jarbawi). The PA sought to dominate civil and security institutions to translate its political agreements with Israel and the international community to concrete and functional control on the ground in the West Bank and Gaza (Awad 2017; Usher 1996; Hilal 2002). It further sought to create a hegemony over civil and security spheres and to undermine the influence of the well-financed and vibrant NGO sector. Finally, it aimed to control individual and public space in face of Islamist political parties that became increasingly popular in the 1990s (Jarbawi 1996; Monshipouri 1996; Shikaki 1996). In this vein, the PA quickly expanded its public sector, hiring a large number of security personnel and incorporating PLO members into its ranks.

Much of the PA's senior leadership consisted of PLO security and civil personnel who were based outside the West Bank and Gaza before the Oslo Accords. The Accords granted 100,000 PLO members (including their families) the right to return to Palestine from the diaspora (primarily Jordan, Lebanon and Tunisia) (Tamari 2002, p. 103).[6] The PA was compelled to absorb the entire bureaucracy of the PLO into the new government, as stipulated in article 44 of its Basic Law of 1994: 'public employees who receive their salaries from the public treasury shall remain in their positions' (Aruri and Carroll 1994, p. 15). With guarantees to receive job security for PLO employees in the new government, the PA imported a large portion of its bureaucratic class into the West Bank and Gaza (author interview with Dua'a Qurie). Palestinian sociologist Jamil Hilal describes this process as a defining moment that fractured Palestinian society. For Hilal, PLO returnees viewed forming the government of the PA as a reward for their political struggles outside Palestine (Hilal 2002; Hilal and Khan 2004). For PLO returnees, employment with the PA represented mere bureaucratic legitimacy for extracting financial benefits after the triumph of their political struggle. Returnees held the bulk of senior ministerial positions and represented more than 25 per cent of posts on the boards of ministers, deputy ministers, and assistant deputy minsters (Amundsen and Ezbidi 2002, p. 22; see also Hilal 2007). In this context, clientelism, patronage and corruption were imported into

---

[6] It is also important to note that the number of total returnees as of 1997 stood at least at 260,000 individuals. For more see Hilal (2007, pp. 11–22).

the nucleus of PA governance (Amundsen and Ezbidi 2004; Jamal 2001; Brynen 1995; Tuastad 2010).

For many Palestinians, governance was transferred to an entire bureaucratic system that not only imported its style of governance but also installed its own elite bureaucratic class. In an effort to quell unease in public sentiment towards the PLO, the PA hired a large number of locals in its security apparatus as well as incorporating the existing (i.e., pre-1993) public sector employees. The PA's attempts at co-optation were wide-ranging, covering both vertical and horizontal societal segments. According to Rubin (1999, p. 17), the PA's co-optation of societal groups included independents, leaders and members of political opposition, civil society members, and even active critics of the PA. Hilal describes the rush for mass public employment as an attempt to dilute the repercussions of importing a ruling class (Hilal 2002; Hilal and Khan 2004, p. 95). It is clear, then, that public employment at large was not only driven by administrative or governance needs. It was, rather, promulgated as an inclusionary mechanism built upon the exchange of political acquiescence with income security to diverse segments of society.

The resulting bureaucratic structure of the PA came to closely resemble rentier classes of traditional rentier states across the Arab world (see, e.g., Beblawi 1987). First, the PA's bureaucratic class received a substantial portion of the government's total expenses, at 60–70 per cent of all public expenditures during the early years of PA's formation (Shu'aybi and Shikaki 2000, pp. 89–90). These sums frequently exceeded all accrued external income to the PA, including foreign aid and clearance revenue. Furthermore, the PA public sector was divided between the security and civil spheres. More than 50 per cent of new employment between 1994 and 2000 was dedicated to the security sector, mirroring the security-centred rentier structure of public employment rampant in the Middle East (Shu'aybi and Shikaki 2000, pp. 89–90; see also Ross 2001, and Chapter 2 of this volume). Second, the PA's public sector was weakly institutionalised and ineffective. The upper echelons of government were orchestrated via patronage, factional loyalty, and deference to political leadership (Amundsen and Ezbidi 2002). Particularly during the early years of the PA, cabinet meetings were not held regularly and were replaced by 'leadership assemblies'. The assemblies typically included ministers, Fatah members, governors, security leaders, and the president's own network of invitees. A PA minister during the 1990s explained: 'Everything of substance had to be liaised with the President where access to see him was controlled by several people who worked in his office'. They added, 'Ministers rarely coordinated with each other, and the cabinet was largely fragmented because each minister managed their own ministry according to their own strategies and perspectives' (author interview with former PA minister, Ramallah, 2017). In this context, neopatrimonialism, centred on Yasser Arafat, was a dominant feature of the public sector, represented by a highly concentrated and personalised presidential power and systematic clientelist networks of influence that exchanged jobs for loyalty and political support.

In recent years, and particularly post the Salam Fayyad institutional reforms, the PA's institutional standards made significant progress in all the sectors of institutionalisation and governance that were measured by the UN (Persson 2018), the EU, the World Bank (2010, 2011a) and the IMF. In 2010, the World Bank stated: 'if the PA maintains its current performance in institution-building and delivery of public services, it is well positioned for the establishment of a state at any point in the near future' (World Bank 2010). The IMF followed suit in 2011 and affirmed that the PA was capable of conducting 'sound economic policies expected of a future well-functioning Palestinian state' (IMF 2011). Additionally, speaking on behalf of the European Union in 2011, then-High Representative for Foreign Affairs and Security Policy, Catherine Ashton, declared: 'The Palestinian Authority has made significant progress on this state-building agenda. Today Palestinian institutions compare favourably with those in established states' (European Union 2011). Although the PA's governance efficiency improved, however, its recruitment process remained marred by nepotism and factional favouritism. Following the ratification of the Civil Service Law in 2005, and immense pressure from the World Bank and IMF on the PA to control the expansion of its wage bill, hiring new public servants had to be approved by multiple officials, including by the Ministry of Finance and Planning. This reduced random hiring practices and capped public employment at 3000 net recruitment per year starting in 2007, followed by a zero-net hiring policy starting in 2013. However, this process was limited to civil servants and excluded hiring in the PA's security sector (World Bank 2011b; author interview with MoFP official, Ramallah, 2017). As many interviewees noted, recruitment and promotion procedures remained under the control of the Ministry of Interior and did not comply with the same rules as the rest of PA public employment.

Overall, the PA maintained patronage and client networks through several avenues. At least 10,000 non-performing security and civil employees remained on the books of the PA's payroll (see, e.g., World Bank 2007). The World Bank (2011b) referred to non-performing employees as employees who received a salary while not working for the PA or while working outside the country. This also included around 2000 individuals on 'temporary contracts', who were appointed at the discretion of ministers or deputy ministers. A corruption watchdog concluded that 'some officials are still appointing people with whom they have a relationship or reserving future positions for them to help them garner financial benefits. This was principally possible because the expert and consultant contracts were still operational in the public sector during 2016' (AMAN 2016). In addition, staff promotion remained largely at the discretion of influential political actors including ministers, governors, the prime minister and the president. In most cases, networks of empowered individuals at the deputy ministerial level held the keys to promotion and hiring decisions. These individuals, some with direct access to the PA president, outlived several ministers and were typically empowered by personalised or familial relations with powerful Fatah members. This underscored the issue of factionalism in the PA, where many new public employees were affiliated primarily with Fatah, which, as Anders Persson explains, 'enforce[d] structures of patronage and clientelism' (Persson 2018).

As such, the PA's institutional improvements transformed the way it co-opted society through its public expenditure. Mass public hiring was restricted and the process increased in complexity and became more exclusive. Donors' conditionalities directly shaped this process and provided the technical assistance and funding to develop the PA's administrative capacity to control its public sector (author interview with UN Official, West Bank, 2017). The changes in PA hiring processes, however, did not translate to a more transparent authority but instead to a more exclusionary one with the potential for significant financial gains. According to Ghada alMadbouh, the resultant mechanism, which rewarded loyalty with high salaries, 'encouraged voluntary co-optation and wider penetration of societal groups' (author interview with Ghada alMadbouh). Majdi Abu Zaid explained: '[H]igh positions inside the PA bring about valuable financial and political privileges that in addition to high financial rewards include free use of a car (or cars), rent-free housing, telephone, protection and assistance personnel, VIP card, and, at times, income tax and custom tax exemptions' (author interview with Majdi Abu Zaid). High positions include ministers and former ministers, Palestinian Legislative Council members, deputy ministers, heads of PA centres or agencies, and heads of security divisions or generals. In addition, PLO members, and PLO returnees, in particular, were generally employed in senior PA positions, and their salaries were high in comparison to regular administrative and labour-intensive positions.

Inequality within the PA's public sector is further evident between different ministries. The two ministries that traditionally received lower salaries than other ministries were health and education. The majority of the 20,000 public employees integrated by the PA from the Israeli civil administration in 1994 were teachers or health workers (Hilal and Khan 2004, p. 72). Their political loyalty and party affiliation did not necessarily belong to the PLO or Fatah (Said and Badawi 2004; see also Kayed 2003; Sbeih and Abu Alia 2002). Within this context, teachers and health workers received relatively low starting salaries and their salaries failed to rise at par with other ministries. This sparred several confrontations between the employees of these ministries and the PA. Public teachers, in particular, orchestrated a series of strikes that started with the inception of the PA.

Palestinian public teachers engaged in a number of harsh confrontations with the PA between 1994 and 2020. On all occasions, strike leaders directed their dissidence not only at the government but also at the union that claimed to represent them (Brown 2003, p. 183). Palestinian teachers in the West Bank and Gaza represented the bulk of public employment under Israel's rule before 1994. When the PA started its operations, it incorporated this entire body of employees and began to slowly fill its ranks with loyal members. In 1993, a plethora of organisations represented teachers; unionisation was banned under Jordanian, Egyptian, and Israeli laws, encouraging them to form Local Committees for political and professional representation (Brand 1988, pp. 38–40). In an attempt to co-opt and control teachers' efforts, the PLO formed the General Union of Palestinian Teachers (GUPT) in 1969. But the GUPT faced daunting hurdles in representing teachers: first, it was based in Tunisia and was banned from operating in the West Bank and Gaza by Israel; and second, the GUPT's factional background and allegiance to Fatah diminished its local appeal (Brand 1988; author interview with member of GUPT). Teachers therefore continued to form Coordinating

Committees inside Palestine. In 1990, Muhammad Suwan, a Jerusalem-based teacher, formed the General Union for Palestinian Teachers in the Occupied Territories (GUPTOT) (Brown 2003, p. 184). The GUPT was imported to the West Bank and Gaza after 1994, but it struggled to gain legitimacy among teachers there, who continued to operate within local Coordinating Committees. The PA managed to co-opt both leaders and many members of the GUPTOT and GUPT by offering hefty salaries and senior positions in various ministries. For example, Jamil Shihada, head of GUPT, accepted a senior position at the Ministry of Interior (Brown 2003, pp. 181–87). Consequently, both organisations' claims to independence were undermined and routinely questioned. As Brown explains, '[u]nion leaders felt caught in a very awkward position, unwilling to confront their patrons in Fatah and the [Palestinian National Authority] but also embarrassed in front of their membership for their meekness' (Brown 2003, p. 182). However, the Coordinating Committees were never truly dissolved and confronted the PA and the co-opted leadership of unions.

The first confrontation between teachers and the PA occurred in 1997. Coordinating Committees led a strike against low wages and high inflation. In an effort to contain teachers, the Ministry of Education offered a mediocre salary increase, citing fiscal difficulties (Brown 2003, p. 184). Consequently, strikes intensified across many locations in the West Bank. The PA relied on the pliable GUPT and GUPTOT to suppress dissidence, eventually managing to obtain a call for the strike to end, but the teachers' Coordinating Committees repudiated their union leaderships' concessions. In what to become a customary tactic for the PA, the security services were called upon to coerce Coordinating Committees leaders and active members. Several leaders were arrested, dismissed from their positions or transferred to rural areas (author interviews, West Bank, 2017). One Coordinating Committee leader recalled: 'security services showed up at teacher's houses and forced them to open schools. A few of my colleagues were arrested, tortured, and forced to sign declarations against the Coordinating Committees and the strike' (author interview, Hebron 2017). The PA fired as many as 18 teachers and detained some Coordinating Committees' leaders without trial (Assaf 2004). In the end, the PA's coercive tactics—a combination of security suppression, institutional punitive measures for leaders and participating teachers, and pressure from co-opted unions—succeeded in curbing the strike with no substantial achievement for teachers.

The strikes were suppressed, but the teachers' struggle with the PA reflected the latter's failure to incorporate the pre-1994 public sector employees. The PA's Ministry of Education and Higher Education (MEHE) had developed two separate compensatory systems for its staff: one for compensating the ministry's administrative and bureaucratic apparatus, and a second for teachers. While the ministry's senior positions and many of its administrative employees were PLO returnees or political appointees, teachers were largely local workers (author interviews with teachers and a senior Ministry of Education and Higher Education member, Ramallah, 2017; see also Roy [2000]). The disparity in salaries and local teachers' exclusion from administrative and senior positions at the MEHE exposed the limitations of the PA attempts to buy off and co-opt social groups organised outside PLO control. It further reflects the complexities of the PA's rentier bargain, with financial compensation not translating to political loyalty.

The 1997 strike gave rise to a more confrontational strike in 2000. Teachers were promised a salary increase in line with compensatory scales implemented in other PA ministries. However, the promised salary increases were not implemented even after the Palestinian Legislative Council passed the Civil Service Law, which promised generous salary increases for teachers. Simultaneously, the PA moved to implement a new pension system that included a deduction of 10 per cent from teachers' salaries. Both policies reignited the role of Coordinating Committees and triggered a number of strikes across the West Bank (Brown 2003, p. 185). The PA refused to meet teachers' demands because it had made commitments to international donors and was under pressure from the World Bank to balance its budget and curb the expansion of its wage bill (author interview with former PA minister, Ramallah, 2017). In 2000, the PA's wage bill had mushroomed to an unsustainable rate of 60 per cent of total expenditure (Iqtait 2020, p. 180). The strike snowballed into a national issue, prompting NGOs, various political parties, Legislative Council members, and members within the PA to pressure the PA to meet teacher's demands. Nonetheless, the PA's inability to fund further increases to its wage bill, coupled with its commitments to meet donor conditions, entrenched its stance (author interview with former PA minister). Security services were again called upon to suppress strikes. Coordinating Committee leaders and members were routinely arrested, threatened, and often tortured. The confrontation persisted for more than three months and only subsided after national confrontations with

120    A. IQTAIT

Israel broke out in May, leading Coordinating Committees to declare that nationalist issues were more important than 'materialistic demands' (Brown 2003, p. 187). Strikes were renewed in September 2000 but were again suspended after the eruption of the second Palestinian Intifada in the same month.

Teachers' strikes against PA policies became a commonplace feature of the public education sector in Palestine. From 2000, the GUPTOT dissolved into the larger and more vocal GUPT where Ahmad Suhwail, GUPT head, consolidated his influence. Teachers routinely clashed with the MEHE, GUPT and the PA in the form of wildcat strikes (Qato and Abu Moghli 2018). More than 50 strikes were organised in the West Bank from 2000 culminating in the longest confrontation between teachers and the PA, in 2016. More than 35,000 teachers initiated a series of sustained strikes across the West Bank, and, unlike previous strikes, the 2016 confrontation witnessed mass horizontal and vertical mobilisation: teachers, school principals and some MEHE personnel participated. Compliance rates exceeded 83 per cent of public schools and teachers and represented the largest public worker mobilisation in the PA's history (Qato and Abu Moghli 2018). The Palestinian government attempted to defuse the situation through the GUPT, which in turn repeatedly called upon teachers to return to work. Notably, 7000 teachers refused to participate in non-GUPT sponsored strikes. Prime Minister Rami Hamdallah famously refused to interact with Coordinating Committee leaders, denouncing their demonstrations as serving 'external political agendas' (Dunia AlWatan 2016). Hamdallah announced that he would only accept the teacher's demands for higher salaries if 'the Palestinian Authority discovers an oil field' (Qato and Abu Moghli 2018). The strikes were called off when President Mahmoud Abbas promised to meet some of the teacher's demands by January 2018. Throughout the two-month confrontation, the PA utilised the security sector to disrupt public events of mass mobilisation. For example, teachers were prevented from travelling to Ramallah on 23 February 2016 when PA security members, in coordination with the Israeli military, installed checkpoints throughout the West Bank (Baker and Sawafta 2016). Teachers were routinely imprisoned, threatened, or co-opted. Some of the Committee leaders were lured by high-paying administrative positions; others were transferred to rural schools, and many were fired (author interviews, West Bank, 2020).

Hamdallah's comments about finding an oil field as a prerequisite for meeting teachers' salary increases was motivated by the fiscal strains of the PA. The World Bank and IMF exercised substantial leverage over the PA's public expenditures. For example, the PA was compelled to limit the number of public employees and commit to a zero-net hiring policy in accordance with World Bank pressures in 2013. Accordingly, the World Bank issued a comprehensive public expenditure review of the PA in September 2016. The report, which was issued only five months after the teachers' strike had been quelled, declared 'the fiscal situation of the Palestinian Authority is not sustainable'. The report blamed the large wage bill of the Palestinian public sector, stating that it was 'among the highest in the world' and represented '55 per cent of recurrent expenditures, and as much as 83 per cent of public revenues'. The World Bank report also criticised the high wages of PA staff, which represented one of the highest relative to GDP per capita in the world (World Bank 2016b, pp. xv–xvi). One PA official recalled that the World Bank's report was a 'reminder to Hamdullah and [Finance Minister Shukri] Bishara that the PA could not afford to meet any of the teachers' demands' (author interview with Ministry of Finance and Planning official, Ramallah, 2017). The World Bank even mentioned the teachers' strike and cited the 'union's bargaining power' as a 'primary reason for driving public remunerations to grow beyond affordable levels' (World Bank 2016b, p. 28). The timing and content of the World Bank's report point to its systematic involvement in shaping the PA's responsiveness to societal demands. A former PA minister interviewed for this research argued: 'complying with the World Bank grants the PA leverage over donor countries. We committed to fiscal tightening pressures because it left the chance open for future increases in aid commitments. When we met fiscal targets, the World Bank praised the PA and that strengthened the reputation of the PA as a fiscally responsible entity' (author interview with former PA minister, Ramallah, 2017).

The PA may have sustained the internal rejections of its rentier contract, but its image and legitimacy within wider society deteriorated. A public poll conducted by the Palestine Centre for Policy and Survey Research in 2016 revealed that 73 per cent of the public believed that teachers' wages were not fair, 75 per cent blamed the PA policies for teachers' strikes, and 84 per cent considered the PA's response to strikes unacceptable (Palestine Centre for Policy and Survey Research 2016). This data provides empirical evidence that the PA's commitments to meet externally imposed fiscal conditionalities undermined its inward accountability and hindered its legitimacy. Teachers' strikes and the PA's responses highlighted the PA's difficulty in navigating a rentier contract with its own public sector. While the previous section explained the role of the multi-rentier structure in the PA's failure to impose its hegemony over the NGO sector, this section has emphasised the failure of the PA to impose a rentier contract over its own rentier class. The PA demanded loyalty in exchange for job security and income, but many felt the need to challenge the inequality within the composition of the public sector. These findings echo recent conclusions reached by Mitchell and Gengler (2018) on the importance of subjective impressions of fairness in the distribution of benefits within rentier classes. Furthermore, despite public teachers' failures to impose their demands, they presented the PA with one of the most significant challenges in its efforts to assert its primacy over Palestinian society.

## 5.4 Dual Rentierism and the Private Sector

The Palestinian Authority became the largest player in the Palestinian economy after 1994. Empirical evidence of this structure was presented in the previous chapter, where government consumption was shown to represent 33 per cent of total GDP. Government consumption relative to GDP more than doubled between 1994 and 2020, and the share of private consumption shrank by 25 per cent during the same period (PCBS n.d.). Rentier states tend to be the most powerful actors in the economy and own most means of production. This dominance allows the state to regulate the role of the private sector through patronage, corruption and nepotism, as discussed in Chapter 2 (see, e.g., Ross 2001, pp. 332–37; Moore 2004, p. 308; Djankov et al. 2008, p. 171). In recent years, rentier states have engaged in entrepreneurial and 'new state capitalist' activity, where the state owns and professionally operates an array of businesses in hydrocarbon and non-hydrocarbon sectors (Gray 2011, pp. 32–33). In Palestine, the PA's attempts to run a similar model of engagement with the local economy can be categorised into two distinct periods: pre- and post-2000.

When the PA started its operations in 1994 it lacked control over means of production, an industrial base, and sovereignty over the territory. The parameters for its involvement in the economy were thus swayed in favour of competing with the existing under-developed local private sector through partial or total ownership of state–private ventures (Haddad 2016, pp. 81–93). Public companies, private monopolies, and oligopolies were established in sectors such as telecommunications, infrastructural services, commercial banks, insurance companies, import monopolies, and energy (Nasr 2004). The vast majority of capital utilised to fund these ventures was sourced from the Palestinian diaspora, where leading wealthy Palestinians such as Abd al-Majid Shoman, Munib al-Masri, Said Khoury and Omar al-Aqqad provided the start-up capital for the PA's ventures (Hilal 2002, pp. 90–98). The return of wealthy Palestinians to the West Bank and Gaza agitated the local business community, and gave rise to a conflictual relationship between 'expatriate' and 'native' capital (Hilal 2002; Tamari 2002, p. 111). While Palestinians abroad had amassed formidable wealth capable of driving large-scale investment in infrastructure and services, local businesses, which were family-based and undercapitalised, were unable to match the capacity and power of expatriate capital. To weather the competition and ensure their survival, local businesses mobilised in regional chambers of commerce and began to lobby the PA for protection and financial incentives (Hilal 2002, pp. 90–98).

The PA's motives for penetrating the local economy were driven by rent creation and societal co-optation. According to Mohamed Nasr (2004, p. 188), 'it was a rational response on the part of the PA in a context where its trade and fiscal opportunities were seriously constrained'. Accordingly, before 2000, the PA routinely relied on its economic enterprises to cover public expenditure costs or finance other patronage activities (author interview with Majdi Abu Zaid). The PA's economic enterprises' revenue was not consolidated or reflected in the Ministry of Finance and Planning's records. Towards the end of 1999 and early 2000, donors pressured the PA to privatise its commercial assets in the spirit of public reform and in order to receive increased foreign aid (Sayigh and Shikaki 1999, p. 22). The PA's compliance came only after the second Intifada and Israel's siege of Arafat's compound in 2002, when the PA agreed to undergo fiscal reforms led by Salam Fayyad. The rationale for the PA's attempt at creating monopolies stemmed from its structural rentier context of the PA and wider Palestinian economy. The Paris Protocol stipulated that clearance revenue would be disbursed only after meeting several technical conditions (Gaza–Jericho Agreement, Annex IV, article VI). These technical conditions involve submitting special-form bills (invoices) to the representatives of each side for tax rebates. Failure to submit these bills by one party meant that this party would not be able to collect the tax rebate on these bills. In the Palestinian case, non-delivery of clearance bills by importers from or though Israel cost the PA treasury hundreds of millions of dollars per year (World Bank 2016a). From the PA's point of view, the best way to minimise these losses and to ensure delivery of clearance bills to the Ministry of Finance and Planning was to control the entire import of certain products or by the creation of monopolies (author interview with Riyad Mousa, Ramallah, 2017; see also Nasr 2004, p. 187). Although PA monopolies were regularly cited as corrupt, they empowered the PA to maintain macroeconomic orthodoxy while providing generous tax incentives for important groups in society, and increase the size of its public sector employment (Fjeldstad and Zagha 2004, p. 209).

However, the fiscal reforms imposed on the PA post-2000 altered its penetration and involvement in running the private sector and its capacity for rent creation or societal co-optation. The PA had very little scope to refuse donors' demands for reform. First, donors played a crucial role in pressuring Israel to resume the flow of clearance revenue after it withheld transfers between 2000 and 2002 (author interview with former PA minister, Ramallah, 2017). Second, the Palestinian economy had suffered massive devastation during the second Intifada and was in dire need of economic and humanitarian support from donors. Raja Khalidi described the involvement of donors and international financial organisations in Palestinian economic and public sector management during this period as an 'international financial trusteeship' (Khalidi 2005, p. 79). A relationship built upon total financial transparency had evolved, which without a doubt motivated donors to continue their lifeline support of the PA in a context of sustained political instability. However, the donors' policies fostered an economic model based on neoliberal ideals, with the central government continuously concerned with maximising revenues, minimising spending and controlling fiscal deficits (author interview with former PA minister).

The business community was directly affected by the PA's economic reforms in two ways. First, native capital, represented by a pre-1994 web of local businessmen and regional chambers of commerce, resorted to rebuilding their networks with Israeli businesses. Having conducted economic activity with Israeli counterparts since 1967, local businesses quickly regained their role as lead suppliers of goods and services to domestic markets post-2000 (author interview with Hanan Taha-Rayyan, Ramallah, 2017). Businesses such as Bakri, Hirbawi, Masrouji Natshe, Qadi, and Zalmout strengthened their cross-border reach with their Israeli counterparts, reshaping old relationships and forming new ones (author interviews, West Bank, 2020). Hanan Taha-Rayyan stressed the importance of local knowledge in the revival of native capital's role in supplying the Palestinian economy: 'Masrouji and others proved that conducting business in Palestine is difficult if you are not well versed in local structures and networks. Many businesses that have served in Palestine since [the] 1970s showed resilience and quickly were able to engage with the domestic markets after the PA lost its control of the private sector' (author interview with Hanan Taha-Rayyan).

Second, expatriate capital continued to dominate the services sector represented by commercial banks, telecommunications, and large-scale construction. As their financial capacity continued to be significant in terms of the Palestinian economy, expatriate businessmen were able to develop high-level relationships with Israeli officials and businesses (author interview with Mahmoud Eljafari, Ramallah 2017). While local businesses relied on grassroots business networks, expatriate businessmen developed bureaucratic and business relationships at the formal and senior levels in Israel. Tariq Dana cites five examples that supported this argument: Rawabi city, the industrial zones, Palestinian investment in Israel and settlements, contracting Israeli security companies, and Palestinian–Israeli partnerships in tech ventures (Dana 2014). According to Dana, these examples provided ample evidence of high-level economic integration between expatriate capital in Palestine and the Israeli economy (Dana 2014).

The example of Rawabi, a planned city in the West Bank, was the most prominent of these evolving interests. The project, run by Palestinian-American businessman Bashar al-Masri, had an estimated value of USD 1.4 billion, and was considered one of the largest private investment projects in Palestine (Booth 2017). Situated in proximity to several Israeli settlements, the city represented the epitome of economic and security cooperation between the Israeli government and Palestinian businessmen (Grandinetti 2015; Sarsar 2015). Professor Mahmoud Eljafari noted that 'Rawabi is a mega-project with a value of more than 10 per cent of the Palestinian economy. The procedural aspects of completing a project of this size in the West Bank are impossible without Israel's approval and involvement'. Accordingly, Eljafari adds: 'A certain class of Palestinian businessmen understood Israel's role in the economy and decided to invest in cooperation with Israeli businesses and leadership' (author interview with Mahmoud Eljafari).

The aforementioned developments affected the PA's ability to co-opt or relate to the business community. On the surface, it could be argued that the PA's official role had been reduced to ensuring that businesses fulfilled their tax obligations. But the machinations of this relationship were more nuanced. First, the PA's fiscal penetration of the private sector was superfluous. With a corporate tax rate of 15–20 per cent (Palestinian Investment Promotion Agency, n.d.(b)), only 2.6 per cent of the PA's total revenue was generated from income taxes payable by corporations (Iqtait 2021, pp. 259–60). Second, medium-sized businesses' interaction with the PA comprised submitting import clearance invoices to the finance ministry in exchange for preferential tax treatment, or quick settlements of financial accounts (Iqtait 2020, 191). Third, large businesses' interaction was simplified to mere accounting duties due to the low corporate tax laws and the considerable economic incentives promulgated in the PA's investment law (Palestinian Investment Promotion Agency, n.d.(a)). Fourth, for the wider business community, this relationship was based on the submission of clearance invoices to the PA and lax implementation of tax collections.

As such, the PA implemented a number of reforms to enhance recoverable revenue rates and convince Palestinian businesses to provide their VAT and custom certificates (the main components of the clearance revenue receipts). The PA created an independent tax unit within the Ministry of Finance and Planning named the 'Large Taxpayer Unit'. The unit was a one-stop shop whereby the PA processed VAT, income tax, customs, and other tax records for 428 Palestinian business establishments under favourable administrative conditions (author interview with Ministry of Finance and Planning officials, Ramallah, 2017). Businesses that ran operational annual budgets of 10 million New Israeli Shekels (about USD 3 million) or more automatically qualified for the 'Large Taxpayer Unit'.[7] One of the main advantages of the Large Taxpayer Unit was that its members had access to the PA's Automated System for Customs Data Analysis (ASYCUDA). ASYCUDA provided comprehensive tax services between the PA and Israel and significantly reduced necessary bureaucratic and administrative steps in submitting Israeli-processed customs and VAT certificates to the PA (author interview with Ministry of Finance and Planning officials, Ramallah, 2017). Businesses

---

[7] The New Israeli Shekel exchange rate against the US dollar fluctuates; the 2021 average was 3.1 ILS per USD.

that did not qualify for the Large Taxpayer Unit complied with different collection procedures. Representatives of these businesses were required to visit several Ministry of Finance and Planning departments in order to issue ASYCUDA analysis certificates and settle their tax receipts (author interview with Ministry of Finance and Planning officials, West Bank, 2017).

The Large Taxpayer Unit accounted for the majority of the PA's revenue, indicating a high rate of dependence on a very small percentage of the tax base. Several PA officials indicated to the author that 85 per cent of the VAT and customs component of clearance revenue originated from the Large Taxpayer Unit (author interview with Ministry of Finance and Planning officials, Ramallah, 2017). Accordingly, the Large Taxpayer Unit accounted for nearly 57 per cent of all clearance revenue, which translates to the Large Taxpayer Unit funding nearly 25 per cent of all PA expenditures. Large taxpayers, then, had institutionalised access to the PA institutions. According to Khalil Shikaki, 'the PA's preferential treatment of [a] small number of businesses has fostered the creation of rentier elites within the business community, and has granted access for a small number of wealthy businesses to the state' (Ramalah, 2017).

Thus, the PA's attempt to enhance recoverable revenue rates from Israel resulted in the creation of rentier reliance and clientelist networks driven by rent-seeking and easy access to PA services. Figure 5.2 displays the importance of Israel in this relationship, in which it acted as both a collector and distributor of rents. Within this framework, Palestinian business elites were granted the opportunity to access international and Israeli markets, by importing products directly and indirectly from international markets or by trading with Israel. Consequently, Israel benefited from this relation by extracting three per cent of the total rents collected from Palestinian traders before handing the total amount to the PA. At the same time, the private sector in Israel benefited from the handling, processing, and transportation of products from Israeli ports to Palestinian areas (Chapter 4). Furthermore, the Israeli private sector created economic surplus from indirect importation practices prevalent among Palestinian traders (Chapter 4).

Similarly, Palestinian businesses relied on the Israeli side for accessing international markets, and the delivery of their products to Palestinian markets. Their relationship with the Israeli side was characterised by an asymmetrical rate of reliance; due to the much larger Israeli economy, Palestinians' economic activity in or with Israel represented a small

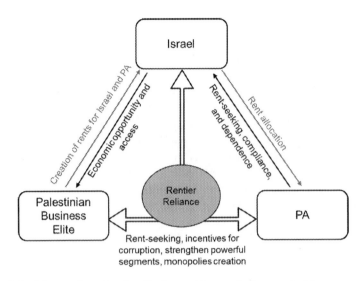

Fig. 5.2 The rentier triangle of reliance (*Source* Author analysis)

share of the larger Israeli economy. Consequently, the economic surplus was dependent on Israel's approval for economic activity to take place through its facilities and markets. Furthermore, the business's relationship with the PA was not consequential for their ability to engage in this economic structure. As explained in Chapter 4, traders needed a simple import licence from the PA in order to import from international markets. This explained the PA's attempt to incentivise businesses through the Large Taxpayer Unit and preferential administrative treatment. However, as many interviewees pointed out to the author, personal favours—in the form of under-reporting of taxes, personal business deals, and access to other tax or state services—occurred regularly within the Large Taxpayer Unit (author interview with the CEO of transparency watchdog, Ramallah, 2017). Finally, the PA was asymmetrically reliant on Israel and business elites for accruing clearance revenue. The PA's lack of influence on the creation or accruing of clearance revenue fostered a state of dependence on Israel on one hand, and on the Palestinian business community on the other hand. Moreover, the PA's preferential treatment of a minority of businesses resulted in further alienation of the majority of the business community. This perpetuated the PA's reliance on the business elites, as they held the keys to securing the PA's most influential source of revenue.

### 5.4.1 Arrears System as a Coercion Mechanism

The arrears system (discussed in Chapter 4) presented the PA with a serious financial challenge, but was also utilised to coerce the business community in an attempt to enhance domestic tax mobilisation. The arrears system was essentially formed because the PA occasionally depended on the private sector to extend a line of credit in the form of goods and services with a non-disclosed compensation date. For example, the Ministry of Health accumulated arrears of USD 193 million in 2013, corresponding to 54 per cent of its total spending (Palestine Health Information Center 2018).

Local businesses engaged in active compliance with the Ministry of Finance and Planning in their quest for compensation. Prior to providing a service to the PA, many businesses might not have submitted clearance invoices or avoided paying corporate and income taxes. But after having entered the arrears system, businesses tended to actively submit clearance invoices and disclose their financial records (Iqtait 2021, pp. 262–63). This change was widely reported during field research in Ramallah, Nablus and Hebron, with local businesses operating in a wide range of sectors such as furniture, pharmaceuticals, food and beverages, carpentry, and construction. This change in behaviour was attributed to 'maximising the possibility that PA will provide compensation, quicker' (Author interview with Ramallah-based business owner, Ramallah, 2017). The active compliance of businesses provided grounds for PA leverage over segments of the business community. However, some businessmen mentioned to the author that refusal to supply the PA within the arrears system could result in punitive measures, such as threats of licence revocation, thorough audits, or delayed payment of existing arrears (author interviews, West Bank, 2020).

Interviews conducted with two senior Ministry of Finance and Planning officials in Ramallah indicated that the arrears consolidation strategy relied on 'moving from oldest to newest', although they admitted that 'at times, personal relations could play a role on who gets paid first'. One official added: 'The PA does provide advance payments for services. The system is based on delayed payment principles, where services are acquired and promises of future payments are issued in the form of promissory notes or other mechanisms' (author interviews with MoFP official, Ramallah, 2017). As such, it was natural for the PA, as the largest consumer in the economy, to acquire goods and services from suppliers. Once in the arrears system, businesses were thoroughly audited for tax compliance.

This section has showcased how conditionalities imposed on the PA by donors and Israel shaped its relationships with the business community. As the PA's role in the private sector shifted from active competition to regulation and oversight, it had to evolve its tactics for co-opting different segments of the business community. Large Palestinian businesses were the segment most likely to escape the PA's direct control, as they engaged directly with Israel in large-scale projects or continued to exploit the services provision sector. This implied that they complied with the PA's lax corporate and income tax laws. Local and import-oriented businesses, however, interacted with the PA at two levels. The first represented the PA's reliance on a small percentage of large businesses to deliver clearance invoices so that it could secure these funds from Israel. The second showcased how the PA exploited the arrears system to co-opt the business community. This analysis points to the PA's constant drive to exploit its rentier structure and create new mechanisms to coerce or co-opt its society.

## 5.5   Conclusion

The relationship between the international community and the Palestinian Authority, on the one hand, and between PA and Israeli clearance revenue on the other, hindered the formation of a stable societal contract between the PA and different segments of Palestinian society. NGOs presented a financial threat to the PA via their direct competition for the same sources of rentier income. The PA's responses proved ineffective in face of donors' efforts to keep NGOs financially strong and impede the PA's attempts to exert hegemony over the sector. The PA's competition with the sector transformed to externally empowered co-optation only when the international donors shifted their priorities in favour of Salam Fayyad's projects. Fayyad also provided the PA with an added level of financial leverage over the sector by maximising clearance revenues recovery rates from Israel. Post-Fayyad, after 2013, donors returned to balancing foreign aid disbursements between the PA and the NGO sector. These policies were shown to hinder the PA's ability to fully absorb the sector—even with clearance revenue resources. Moreover, the sector's historical importance in the Palestinian context meant that the PA's inability to dominate it was a symbolic indication of the limitations of the PA's influence over wider Palestinian society.

The most symbolic challenge to the PA's control over Palestinian society emerged from within its rentier class. As was the case with NGOs, inherited economic variables, as well as historical and political factors, curtailed the PA's ability to create a rentier contract with its own rentier class. Public teachers' dissatisfaction with the PA's unequal and politically driven compensatory policies resulted in widespread rejection of the rentier contract on offer. This chapter revealed that the PA's attempts to centralise power through mass co-optation had mixed results. In the early 2000s, a rentier bargain built upon the PA's ability to provide *pane e circus* in exchange for political loyalty did not manifest. In part, the PA's failure to cement its hegemony and use its leverage to manipulate or coerce society undermined its domestic legitimacy. Inequality within the PA's own rentier class further eroded its legitimacy. Job security and salaries did not automatically translate to political loyalty.

As the PA attempted to co-opt the teachers' unions' leadership, teachers resorted to historical mobilisation tactics that were often used before the establishment of the PA. These tactics proved influential in challenging the PA's coercion strategies, as it utilised its bureaucracy or repression apparatus in quelling teacher's mobilisation. Donors played an instrumental role in shaping the PA's responsiveness to teachers' demands. A combination of externally enforced policies and topical technical reports by the IMF and the World Bank kept the PA under close oversight. While teacher's strikes often resulted in very little financial gain, they demonstrate that the PA failed to co-opt its own public sector and to draw a form of a rentier contract with its society.

The PA's effort to penetrate another significant force in the Palestinian political economy was also undermined by the involvement of donors and the clearance revenue mechanism. The PA was forced to curtail its involvement in the private sector, leaving a vacuum that was filled by domestic businesses. The PA was shown to interact in two distinct ways with the local economy: the first was a light level of engagement via simple corporate and income tax extraction from the international investors who had invested in viable sectors in the economy such as infrastructure, telecommunications and commercial banking; the second involved extensive engagement with the local business sector in an effort to collect clearance invoices and promote wider tax compliance. The chapter also detailed how the PA evolved new methods to co-opt the local business community through the arrears system. This case provided insights into the PA's strategy of balancing two separate conditionality mechanisms: the donors' oversight of public records, and Israel's procedural conditions for transferring clearance revenue.

Ultimately, this chapter argued that the PA's commitments to abide by externally imposed conditionalities undermined its inward accountability and hindered its legitimacy. It further shifted the PA's accountability in favour of rent providers. The resultant state–society relationship was weak and plagued by authoritarianism, lack of political institutions, mistrust, and competition. An evolution of a social contract based on taxation and representation was further undermined by the PA's weak domestic legitimacy.

## References

Al-Barghouthi, Samar. 2009. *The Characteristics of the Palestinian Political Elite Before and After the Establishment of the Palestinian National Authority.* Beirut: Al-Zaytouna Centre.

AMAN (Coalition for Accountability and Integrity). 2016. *Integrity and Combating Corruption—2016.* Ramallah: AMAN. https://www.aman-palest ine.org/en/reports-and-studies/1397.html.

Amundsen, Inge, and Basem Ezbidi. 2002. *Clientelist Politics: State Formation and Corruption in Palestine 1994–2000.* Chr. Michelsen Institute Development Studies and Human Rights. https://brage.bibsys.no/xmlui/bitstream/handle/11250/2435883/Report%20R%202002-17.pdf?sequence=2&isAllo wed=y, accessed 10 May 2018.

Amundsen, Inge, and Basem Ezbidi. 2004. 'PNA Political Institutions and the Future of State Formation.' In *State Formation in Palestine: Viability and Governance During a Social Transformation,* edited by Mushtaq Khan, George Giacaman, and Inge Amundsen, 141–67. London: Routledge.

Angrist, Joshua D. 1996. 'Short-Run Demand for Palestinian Labor.' *Journal of Labor Economics* 14, no. 3: 425–53.

Aruri, Naseer. 1994. 'Oslo and the Crisis in Palestinian Politics.' *Middle East International* 467, 17.

Aruri, Naseer H., and John J. Carroll. 1994. 'A New Palestinian Charter.' *Journal of Palestine Studies* 23, no. 4: 15.

Assaf, Omar. 2004. *The Palestinian Public Teachers Movement in the West Bank.* Ramallah: Muwatin, Palestinian Institute for the Study of Democracy [in Arabic].

Atia, Mona, and Catherine Herrold. 2018. 'Governing Through Patronage: The Rise of NGOs and the Fall of Civil Society in Palestine and Morocco.'

*VOLUNTAS: International Journal of Voluntary and Nonprofit Organizations* 29, no. 5: 1044–54.

Awad, Samir. 2017. 'Civil Society in Palestine.' In *Between State and Non-State: Politics and Society in Kurdistan-Iraq and Palestine*, edited by Gülistan Gürbey, Sabine Hofmann, and Ferhad Ibrahim Seyder, 167–69. New York, NY: Palgrave Macmillan.

Ayed, Khalid. 1998. *Palestinian Intifada: The Internal Dimension*. Amman: Dar Al-Shuroq.

Baconi, Tareq. 2018. *Hamas Contained: The Rise and Pacification of Palestinian Resistance*. Stanford, CA: Stanford University Press.

Baker, Luke, and Ali Sawafta. 2016. 'West Bank Teachers' Strike Leaves 500,000 Children at Home for Weeks.' *Reuters*, 11 March. https://www.reuters.com/article/us-palestinians-teachers-idUSKCN0WC1L0, accessed 10 July 2018.

Beblawi, Hazem. 1987. 'The Rentier State in the Arab World.' In *The Rentier State: Nation, State and the Integration of the Arab World*, edited by Hazem Beblawi and Giacomo Luciani, Chapter 2. London: Croom Helm.

Bennett, Adam, and Karim Nashashibi. 2003. 'Transcript of a Press Briefing on the West Bank and Gaza.' International Monetary Fund, 20 September. https://www.imf.org/en/News/Articles/2015/09/28/04/54/tr030920, accessed 1 July 2018.

Booth, William. 2017. 'The $1.4 Billion Bet on a New Palestinian Future.' *Washington Post*, 25 May. https://www.washingtonpost.com/graphics/world/occupied/palestinian-metropolis-rawabi-rises-in-west-bank-as-israeli-occupation-turns-50/?utm_term=.a02a58f5cfc0, accessed 10 October 2018.

Brand, Laurie. 1988. *Palestinians in the Arab World: Institution Building and the Search for State*. New York, NY: Columbia University Press.

Brown, Nathan. 2003. *Palestinian Politics After the Oslo Accords: Resuming Arab Palestine*. Berkeley, CA: University of California Press.

Brynen, Rex. 1995. 'The Neopatrimonial Dimension of Palestinian Politics.' *Journal of Palestine Studies* 25, no. 1: 23–36.

Brynen, Rex. 1996. 'Buying Peace? A Critical Assessment of International Aid to the West Bank and Gaza.' *Journal of Palestine Studies* 25, no. 3: 85.

Brynen, Rex. 2000. *A Very Political Economy*. Washington, DC: United States Institute of Peace Press.

Bulmer, Elizabeth Ruppert. 2003. 'The Impact of Israeli Border Policy on the Palestinian Labor Market.' *Economic Development and Cultural Change* 51, no. 3: 657–76.

Challand, Benoit. 2009. *Palestinian Civil Society: Foreign Donors and the Power to Promote and Exclude*. London: Routledge.

Curmi, Brigitte. 2002. 'Les enjeux de l'après-Oslo. Le mouvement associatif dans les Territoires palestiniens.' In *Pouvoir et associations dans le monde arabe*, edited by Sarah Nefissa. Paris: CNRS Editions.

Dana, Tariq. 2014. 'The Palestinian Capitalists That Have Gone Too Far.' *AlShabaka*, 14 January. https://al-shabaka.org/briefs/palestinian-capitalists-have-gone-too-far/, accessed 20 April 2018.

Dana, Tariq. 2015. 'The Symbiosis Between Palestinian "Fayyadism" and Israeli "Economic Peace": The Political Economy of Capitalist Peace in the Context of Colonisation.' *Conflict, Security & Development* 15, no. 5: 455–77.

Djankov, Simeon, Jose Montalvo, and Marta Reynal-Querol. 2008. 'The Curse of Aid.' *Journal of Economic Growth* 13, no. 3: 169–94.

Dunia AlWatan. 2016. 'Prime Minister in Frank Discussion with Dunia AlWatan.' *Alwatanvoice*, 26 February. https://www.alwatanvoice.com/arabic/news/2016/02/26/875887.html, accessed 10 September 2018.

European Union. 2011. 'High Representative Catherine Ashton Remarks, Brussels, 13 April.' https://www.consilium.europa.eu/uedocs/cms_data/docs/pressdata/EN/foraff/121525.pdf, accessed 14 December 2018.

Farsakh, Leila. 2002. 'Palestinian Labor Flows to the Israeli Economy: A Finished Story?' *Journal of Palestine Studies* 32, no. 1: 13–27.

Fjeldstad, Odd-Helge, and Adel Zagha. 2004. 'Taxation and State Formation in Palestine 1994–2000.' In *State Formation in Palestine: Viability and Governance during a Social Transformation*, edited by Mushtaq Khan, George Giacaman, and Inge Amundsen, 192–214. London: Routledge.

Gaza–Jericho Agreement, Annex IV (29 April 1994) *Protocol on Economic Relations between the Government of the State of Israel and the P.L.O., representing the Palestinian People*, article VI 'Indirect Taxes on Local Production'.

Gerster, Karin A. 2013. 'Palestinian Non-Governmental Organizations: Their Socio-Economic, Social and Political Impact on Palestinian Society.' *Luxemberg Stiftung*. http://rosaluxemburg.ps/wp-content/uploads/2015/03/201 3Palestinian-Non-Governmental-Organizations-English.pdf, accessed 27 April 2018.

Grandinetti, Tina. 2015. 'The Palestinian Middle Class in Rawabi: Depoliticizing the Occupation.' *Alternatives: Global, Local, Political* 40, no. 1: 63–78.

Gray, Matthew. 2011. *A Theory of 'Late Rentierism' in the Arab States of the Gulf*. Georgetown University School of Foreign Service in Qatar Occasional Paper No. 7. Georgetown University.

Haddad, Toufic. 2016. *Palestine LTD: Neoliberalism and Nationalism in the Occupied Territory*. London: I.B. Tauris.

Hammami, Rema. 2000. 'Palestinian NGOs Since Oslo: From NGO Politics to Social Movements?' *Middle East Report 214*, 17.

Hammami, Rema, Jamil Hilal, and Salim Tamari. 2001. *Civil Society in Palestine: Case Studies*. European University Institute Working Paper 2001/36. https://cadmus.eui.eu/handle/1814/1745.

Hanafi, Sari, and Linda Tabar. 2003. 'The Intifada and the Aid Industry: The Impact of the New Liberal Agenda on the Palestinian NGOs.' *Comparative Studies of South Asia, Africa and the Middle East* 23, nos. 1 & 2: 205–14.

Hilal, Jamil. 2002. *The Formation of the Palestinian Elite: From the Emergence of the National Movement to the Establishment of the National Authority.* Ramallah and Amman: Muwatin and al-Urdun al-Jadid [in Arabic].

Hilal, Jamil. 2007. *Assessing the Impact of Migration on Palestinian Society in the West Bank and Gaza.* CARIM Research Reports 2007/02. Robert Shuman Centre for Advanced Studies, European University Institute.

Hilal, Jamil, and Mushtaq Khan. 2004 'State Formation Under the PNA.' In *State Formation in Palestine: Viability and Governance During a Social Transformation,* edited by Mushtaq Khan, George Giacaman, and Inge Amundsen, 64–120. London: Routledge.

ICBS. 1996. *National Accounts of Judea, Samaria and the Gaza Area 1968–1993.* Special Report No. 1012. Jerusalem: ICBS.

International Monetary Fund. 2011. *Program Note: West Bank and Gaza.* https://www.imf.org/external/np/country/notes/wbg.htm, accessed 10 December 2018.

Iqtait, Anas. 2019. 'The Political Economy of Taming the Palestinian Authority.' In *Palestine: Past and Present,* edited by Tristan Dunning, 145–75. Nova Publishing.

Iqtait, Anas. 2020. 'The Political Economy of Rentierism of the Palestinian Authority.' PhD diss., The Australian National University.

Iqtait, Anas. 2021. 'The Palestinian Authority Political Economy: The Architecture of Fiscal Control.' In *Political Economy of Palestine,* edited by Alaa Tartir et al., 249–70. Cham: Palgrave Macmillan.

Jamal, Amal. 2001. 'State-Building, Institutionalization and Democracy: The Palestinian Experience.' *Mediterranean Politics* 6, no. 3: 8–9.

Jarbawi, Ali. 1996. 'Palestinian Politics at a Crossroads.' *Journal of Palestine Studies* 25, no. 4: 29–39.

Jarrar, Allam. 2005 'The Palestinian NGO Sector: Development Perspectives.' *Palestine-Israel Journal of Politics, Economics and Culture* 12, no. 1. https://pij.org/articles/324/the-palestinian-ngo-sector-development-perspectives.

Kayed, Aziz. 2003. *Public Sector Employment Practices Within the PNA.* Ramallah: The Palestinian Independent Commission for Citizens' Rights.

Khalidi, Raja. 2005. 'Reshaping Palestinian Economic Policy Discourse: Putting the Development Horse before the Governance Cart.' *Journal of Palestine Studies* 34, no. 3: 79.

Labib, Taher. 1992. 'The Relationship between Democratization and Arab Civil Society.' In *Civil Society in the Arab World,* edited by Saed Al-Alawi. Beirut: Center for Research of Arab Unity.

Merz, Sibille. 2012. '"Missionaries of the New Era": Neoliberalism and NGOs in Palestine.' *Race & Class* 54, no. 1: 59.

Mitchell, Jocelyn Sage, and Justin J. Gengler. 2018. 'What Money Can't Buy: Wealth, Inequality, and Economic Satisfaction in the Rentier State.' *Political Research Quarterly* 72, no. 1: 1–15.

Monshipouri, Mahmood. 1996. 'The PLO Rivalry with Hamas: The Challenge of Peace, Democratization and Islamic Radicalism.' *Middle East Policy* 4, no. 3: 84–105.

Moore, Mick. 2004. 'Revenues, State Formation, and the Quality of Governance in Developing Countries.' *International Political Science Review* 25, no. 3: 197–319.

Murphy, Francois, and Arshad Mohammed. 2007. 'Donors Pledge $7.4 Billion to Palestinians.' *Reuters*, 17 December. https://www.reuters.com/article/us-palestinians-donors/donors-pledge-7-4-billion-to-palestinians-idUSL1670303120071217?feedType=RSS&feedName=topNews&rpc=22&sp=true, accessed 15 July 2018.

Muslih, Muhammad. 1993. 'Palestinian Civil Society.' *Middle East Journal* 47, no. 2: 258–74.

Nasr, Mohamed. 2004. 'Monopolies and the PNA.' In *State Formation in Palestine: Viability and Governance During a Social Transformation*, edited by Mushtaq Khan, George Giacaman, and Inge Amundsen, 168–89. London: Routledge.

NGO Development Center. 2015. *The Palestinian NGOs Code of Conduct* (second edition). http://www.ndc.ps/code-compliance-mechanism, accessed 7 April 2018.

NGO Development Center. 2020. *Annual Report 2020*. https://www.ndc.ps/sites/default/files/2020-NDC-AR-English.pdf.

Office of the Special Coordinator in the Occupied Territories. 1999. *Rule of Law Development in the West Bank and Gaza Strip Survey and State of the Development Effort*. Brussels: United Nations.

Ophir, Adi, Michal Givoni, and Sari Hanafi. 2009. *The Power of Inclusive Exclusion: Anatomy of Israeli Rule in the Occupied Palestinian Territories*. Brooklyn, NY: Zone Books.

Organisation for Economic Co-operation and Development. 2008. *The Paris Declaration on Aid Effectiveness and the Accra Agenda for Action*. http://www.oecd.org/dac/effectiveness/34428351.pdf.

Palestine Centre for Policy and Survey Research. 2016. *Palestinian Public Opinion Poll No 59*. http://www.pcpsr.org/en/node/636.

Palestine Health Information Center. 2018. *Health Annual Report*. https://www.site.moh.ps/index/Books/BookType/2/Language/ar.

5 THE SOCIETAL LEGACY OF DUAL RENTIERISM 137

Palestine National Authority. 2009. *Program of the Thirteenth Government: Palestine: Ending the Occupation, Establishing the State.* https://unispal.un.org/pdfs/PA_EndingOccupation-Statehood.pdf.

Palestinian Central Bureau of Statistics (PCBS). n.d. 'National Accounts Variables in Palestine for the Years 1994–2020 at Current Prices.' http://www.pcbs.gov.ps/site/lang__en/741/default.aspx.

Palestinian Central Bureau of Statistics (PCBS). 2017. 'The Commission of Detainees and Ex-Detainees Affairs and Palestinian Prisoners Club and the Palestinian Central Bureau of Statistics.' Press release, 17 April. http://www.pcbs.gov.ps/site/512/default.aspx?lang=en&ItemID=1905.

Palestinian Central Bureau of Statistics (PCBS). 2022. Palestinian Labour Force Survey Annual Report: 2021. Ramallah – Palestine. https://www.pcbs.gov.ps/Downloads/book2605.pdf.

Palestinian Centre for Human Rights. 2015. 'Council of Ministers in Ramallah Approves New Restrictions on Non-Profit Companies: PCHR Calls for Abolishing the Decision and Reconsidering the Regulation According to International Standards, Reference 41/2015.' Press release, 9 July. https://pchrgaza.org/en/?p=1502.

Palestinian Investment Promotion Agency. n.d.(a). *Incentives.* http://www.pipa.ps/page.php?id=1c2315y1843989Y1c2315.

Palestinian Investment Promotion Agency. n.d.(b). *Income Tax Law No. 8 of 2011.* http://www.pipa.ps/page.php?id=1bc27fy1819263Y1bc27f.

Pannier, Dominique. 1996. *West Bank and Gaza Civil Service Study, Presentation and Technical Assistance Supervision.* World Bank Memorandum. Washington, DC: World Bank.

Persson, Anders. 2018. 'Palestine at the End of the State-Building Process: Technical Achievements, Political Failures.' *Mediterranean Politics* 23, no. 4: 433–52.

Qato, Mezna, and Mai Abu Moghli. 2018. *A Brief History of a Teacher's Strike.* Middle East Research and Information Project. https://merip.org/2018/06/a-brief-history-of-a-teachers-strike/.

Ross, Michael L. 2001. 'Does Oil Hinder Democracy.' *World Politics* 53, 332–37.

Roy, Sara. 2000. 'The Crisis Within: The Struggle for Palestinian Society.' *Critique: Journal for Critical Studies of the Middle East* 9, no. 17: 9.

Roy, Sara. 2001. 'Palestinian Society and Economy: The Continued Denial of Possibility.' *Journal of Palestine Studies* 30, no. 4: 5–20.

Roy, Sara. 2011. *Hamas and Civil Society in Gaza: Engaging the Islamist Social Sector.* Princeton, NJ: Princeton University Press.

Rubin, Barry. 1999. *The Transformation of Palestinian Politics: From Revolution to State-Building.* Cambridge, MA: Harvard University Press.

Said, Nader, and Walid Badawi. 2004. *Public Administration in the West Bank & Gaza: Obstacles and Opportunities.* Conference paper, InnovMed Consultative Meeting on Priorities in Innovating Governance and Public Administration in the Euro-Mediterranean Region. http://citeseerx.ist.psu.edu/viewdoc/download;jsessionid=0478E58214C654471076AB08821DAF4C?doi=10.1.1.537.7461&rep=rep1&type=pdf.

Sarsar, Saliba. 2015. 'A New Kind of Palestinian Business Leadership.' *International Leadership Journal 7*, no. 2: 67–80.

Sayigh, Yezid, and Khalil Shikaki. 1999. *Strengthening Palestinian Public Institutions.* Council on Foreign Relations.

Sbeih, Majed, and Mamoun Abu Alia. 2002. *Characteristics of the Employees in Public and Private Sectors.* Ramallah: Palestinian Bureau of Statistics.

Schwartz, Alta. 2004. 'The Leadership Role of Palestinian Non-Governmental Organizations: Managing Chaos, Creating Civil Society.' *International Journal of Civil Society Law 2*, no. 2: 63–73.

Shikaki, Khalil. 1996. 'The Peace Process, National Reconstruction, and the Transition to Democracy in Palestine.' *Journal of Palestine Studies 25*, no. 2: 5–20.

Shu'aybi, Azmi, and Khalil Shikaki. 2000. 'A Window on the Workings of the PA: An Inside View.' *Palestine Studies 30*, no. 1: 89–90.

Sullivan, Denis J. 1996. 'NGOs in Palestine: Agents of Development and Foundation of Civil Society.' *Journal of Palestine Studies 25*, no. 3: 94.

Sullivan, Denis J. 2001. *The World Bank and the Palestinian NGO Project: From Service Delivery to Sustainable Development.* Jerusalem: Palestinian Academic Society for the Study of International Affairs.

Tamari, Salim. 2002. 'Who Rules Palestine.' *Journal of Palestine Studies 31*, no. 4: 102–13.

Taraki, Lisa. 1989. 'The Islamic Resistance Movement in the Palestinian Uprising.' *Middle East Report 156*, 30–32.

Tuastad, Dag. 2010. 'The Role of International Clientelism in the National Factionalism of Palestine.' *Third World Quarterly 31*, no. 5: 792–96.

USAID West Bank & Gaza. 2007. *Updated Anti-Terrorism Procedures: Update to Mission Order #21.* USAID 2007-WBG-26. https://www.usaid.gov/sites/default/files/documents/1883/2007-WBG-26.pdf.

Usher, Graham. 1996. 'The Politics of Internal Security: The PA's New Intelligence Services.' *Journal of Palestine Studies 25*, no. 2: 21–34.

World Bank. 1994. *Emergency Assistance Program for the Occupied Territories.* Washington, DC: World Bank.

World Bank. 1997. *Proposed Trust Fund Grant for The Palestinian NGO Project.* Washington, DC: World Bank.

World Bank. 2007. *West Bank and Gaza: Public Expenditure Review.* Report No. 38207-WBG. Washington, DC: World Bank.

World Bank. 2010. *Economic Monitoring Report to the Ad Hoc Liaison Committee: The Underpinnings of the Future Palestinian State: Sustainable Growth and Institutions.* http://siteresources.worldbank.org/INTWESTBA NKGAZA/Resources/WorldBankSep2010AHLCReport.pdf.

World Bank. 2011a. *Economic Monitoring Report to the Ad Hoc Liaison Committee: Building the Palestinian State: Sustaining Growth, Institutions, and Service Delivery.* http://siteresources.worldbank.org/INTWESTBANKG AZA/Resources/AHLCReportApril2011.pdf.

World Bank. 2011b. *Improving Governance and Reducing Corruption.* Washington, DC: World Bank. http://documents.worldbank.org/curated/en/ 135081468329421725/West-Bank-and-Gaza-Improving-governance-and-reducing-corruption.

World Bank. 2016a. 'Palestinian Authority Incurs US$285 Million in Annual Fiscal Losses.' Press release, 18 April. http://www.worldbank.org/en/news/ press-release/2016/04/18/palestinian-authority-incurs-us285-million-in-ann ual-fiscal-losses.

World Bank. 2016b. *Public Expenditure Review of the Palestinian Authority: Towards Enhanced Public Finance Management and Improved Fiscal Sustainability.* http://documents.worldbank.org/curated/en/320891473688227 759/Public-Expenditure-Review-Palestinian-territories.

CHAPTER 6

# Rents, Revenue, and Sovereignty

**Abstract** The concluding chapter outlines the main contributions of the book and areas for further research. The main conclusion of the book is that decades of external economic development programs and Israeli economic policies have left the Palestinian Authority doubly dependent on external income in the form of foreign aid and clearance revenue. This has provided leverage for different actors and forces in the political economy to directly influence the state and its ability to co-opt and coerce. The conditions imposed by rent providers meant that the PA was continually balancing two separate conditionality mechanisms. The first involved technical conditionalities, whereby foreign donors and Israel forced the PA to take procedural steps in order to qualify for rent disbursements. The second mechanism comprised a set of political conditionalities imposed by comprehensive economic, political and security policies. Conditionalities and inconsistent rents windfall altered the accountability of the PA in favour of rent providers, resulting in weak state–society relations and a limited capacity to co-opt society. Finally, continual competition between the PA and the NGO sector over foreign aid fragmented services provision and created parallel governance units. Internally, PA ministries competed for legitimacy with foreign donors, resulting in fragmented and overlapping decision-making governance structures.

© The Author(s), under exclusive license to Springer Nature Switzerland AG 2023
A. Iqtait, *Funding and the Quest for Sovereignty in Palestine*,
https://doi.org/10.1007/978-3-031-19478-8_6

141

**Keywords** Political conditionalities · Technical conditionalities · Rentierism · Clearance revenue mechanism · Foreign aid · Donors · Co-optation · Social contact · Sovereignty

## 6.1 Introduction

The composition of state revenue influences states' policies, state–society relations and the wider economy. In particular, states that rely on political rents for the majority of their revenue suffer a broad set of political and economic consequences. But, as explained in this book, consideration of historical and structural variables, international relations dynamics, the role of different rent types, and policies of rent providers are also pertinent in assessing the true impacts of rents. This book explored the effects of political rents dependency on the Palestinian Authority's policies—including economic policy, state–society relations and foreign policy—between 1994 and 2016. It further identified foreign aid and clearance revenue—the two main components of the PA's revenue—as two sources of political rents accruing to the PA. It utilised a political economy framework extrapolated from Rentier State Theory (RST) to study the effects of political rents.

Although RST has primarily been examined in the context of natural resource-based rentier states, it can also be applied in situations where the state derives large portions of its revenue from political rents. The body of literature closest to understanding the effects of political rents is generally limited to describing the political and economic consequences of foreign aid. However, foreign aid is not the only source of political rents, and many states accrue a significant portion of their income from revenue controlled by other states. The PA accrued most of its income from the Israeli-controlled clearance revenue and from foreign aid. The relationship between foreign aid and the PA's policies has been researched by many, but the dynamics of this relationship with regard to the PA's wider revenues are little understood, and no in-depth examination of the PA budget's components has been conducted. As such, this book identified these theoretical and empirical gaps and set out to conceptualise a framework derived from RST to test the impact of different sources of political rents on the PA's economic policy and state–society relations.

In doing so, the book compared the characteristics of political rents and natural resource rents from the point view of the accruing state. It argued that political rents and natural resource rents are fungible, in that their flow replaces other forms of revenue for the state, thus increasing the dependence of the state on rents and reducing the importance of other sources of potential revenue such as taxation. However, political rents were shown to be a more conditional and less consistent revenue source than natural resource rents. Political rents are highly subject to the preferences of rent providers (which may include internal political objectives or foreign policy orientations), which may attach conditions that dictate the continued flow of rents. These conditions were shown to be tools of exerting influence for economic, political or strategic considerations. Finally, political rents were also found to alter the accountability of the state in favour of rent providers. This included political and economic transparency with rent providers in the form of public financial records management, economic data, and political agreements.

## 6.2 Effects of the PA's Dual Rentierism

The book reveals that the Palestinian economy and public revenues in the West Bank and Gaza have historically been shaped by Israel's political and economic policies and have disproportionately relied on multiple sources of rentier income. It establishes that the PA suffers from a case of dual rentierism: it is dependent on two sources of political rents, in the form of foreign aid and clearance revenue. Rents affected the economic character of the Palestinian economy and undermined the PA's ability to formulate sound economic policy or raise domestic taxes. The book further argues that the PA's dual rentierism stalled efforts to establish a social contract with Palestinian society.

An interplay of political and historical dynamics shaped the availability and type of external income in the West Bank and Gaza through different time periods. For example, the influx of Palestinian workers to Israel after its occupation of the West Bank and Gaza in 1967 resulted in large windfalls of remittances and the absorption of nearly half the labour force. Similarly, the signing of the Oslo Accords ushered in large windfalls of foreign aid that, at times, represented nearly 50 per cent of GDP. Many of the prevalent economic pathologies in the Palestinian economy, including a weak productive sector, excessive unemployment, high levels of local consumption and a volatile macroeconomic environment, are embedded in an inherited economic structure characterised by an excessive reliance on external income in the form of foreign aid and remittances that evolved under Israel's control between 1968 and 1993.

While hopes of sustainable economic growth were high following the signing of the Oslo Accords and the Paris Protocol of 1994, this book has detailed that the Palestinian economy continued to rely excessively on external income for growth. As a result, Dutch Disease symptoms became prevalent in all sectors of the Palestinian economy. From 1994, most employment generation occurred in the public sector, while the agriculture sector and industrial activity withered. Rents enabled unsustainable increases in labour and capital costs relative to per capita income, further eroding the economy's capacity to generate growth or employment in the productive sectors. While the wider political environment of Israeli occupation was germane, the economic consequences of rent dependency could not have been averted. Donor-driven economic development plans further entrenched rent dependency and created a rentier paradox for the Palestinian economy: while rents were essential for sustaining the economy, they further eroded the economy's ability to generate growth independent of external income and thus perpetuated rentier dependency.

The fiscal character of the West Bank and Gaza was also predominantly defined by external revenue even before the creation of the PA. The fiscal skeleton of the Israeli military government between 1967 and 1993 largely resembled that of the PA's budget after 1994. Both budgets were mostly composed of custom duties, taxes deducted from Palestinian labour in Israel, indirect taxes and foreign aid transfers. Israel's continued control over the collection and processing of custom duties, and donors' control over foreign aid disbursements, resulted in around 75 per cent of the PA's total budget falling outside of its direct control. In turn, the PA's fixation on securing clearance revenue and attracting foreign aid undermined its domestic tax collection efforts and hindered its ability to formulate independent economic policy. Rents provided the PA with financial security that ensured its political survival with very little tax mobilisation. This translated to a lack of political will by PA officials to raise taxes from domestic sources. In addition, tax collection mechanisms were insufficient at two levels. The procedural level was characterised by weak follow-up procedures with existing taxpayers, fragile monitoring of unregistered taxpayers and the absence of tax verifications methods, such as field inspections. Ineffectiveness at the structural level was characterised by weak communication and coordination between different tax departments, lack of professional training and deficient tax collection infrastructure.

In addition, the clearance revenue mechanism prevented the PA from exerting a monopoly over Palestinian fiscal revenues. The mechanism also granted Israel de facto control over the essential trade process with Israeli and international markets, and resulted in significant fiscal leakages for the PA. This fostered a divide between the PA and Palestinian traders and fortified pre-PA economic links between Palestinian and Israeli traders, as well as between Palestinian traders and the Israeli government. The book further argued that the PA's dual rentierism, as well as the wider rentier context of the Palestinian economy, enabled a structural dependence on rents. Under current circumstances, the PA's only means of expanding its fiscal revenue hinges on its ability to secure higher rent windfalls for the wider economy. Foreign aid and remittances fund a trade imbalance built upon excessive imports, which in turn fund the PA's main revenues in the form of clearance revenue and budgetary support.

This book argued that the relationship between donors and the Palestinian Authority on the one hand, and between the PA and Israeli clearance revenue on the other, hindered the formation of a stable social contract between the PA and different segments of Palestinian society. Instead, the PA was shown to have evolved authoritarian tendencies, created a fragmented rentier class, and exhibited weak domestic legitimacy.

The book investigated three influential segments of Palestinian society, each situated differently relative to the PA's rentier income: the NGO sector; the PA's own public sector; and the private sector. The NGO sector was a direct competitor of the PA for foreign aid disbursements, while the PA's public sector was the main beneficiary of its rentier structure, with at least 50 per cent of all PA expenditure allocated to its wage bill. Finally, the business community's import activity with or through Israel funded the clearance revenue mechanism.

Rents played an instrumental role in influencing the evolving relationship between the PA and NGO sector. Foreign aid, through its multi-disbursement mechanisms, provided donors with leverage to empower or exclude the PA or the NGO sector. This eroded the PA's ability to co-opt or coerce the NGO sector and further undermined its domestic legitimacy. In addition, the PA's fixation with centralising foreign aid and controlling the NGO sector resulted in constant mistrust and competition. The PA managed to exert partial hegemony over the sector between

2007 and 2013. Salam Fayyad's reforms succeeded in consolidating the PA's fiscal position by securing constant flows of clearance revenue as well as convincing donors to operate through the PA's budget. Consequently, the PA enjoyed an externally empowered hegemony over the NGO sector, albeit a hegemony due to donors' shifting preferences rather than to any extension of PA's local legitimacy.

Teachers' strikes presented the PA with a symbolic challenge that underlined its inability to establish a rentier contract with its own public sector. Although the sector was well paid relative to local and international standards, public teachers rejected the PA's rentier bargain and, on several occasions, launched lengthy rent-seeking movements. The PA's accommodation of their remands was limited, as donors imposed very strict fiscal guidelines that constrained the PA's ability to increase salaries or hire more workers. Viewing the teachers' strikes as a threat, the PA resorted to repressive tactics by forcibly quelling demonstrations, intimidating participating teachers and detaining strike leaders.

The PA's relationship with the business community was also largely shaped by the conditionalities imposed on the PA by donors and Israel. Donors' reforms curbed the PA's ability to run state-owned enterprises in the private sector and restricted its market penetration to taxation and regulation. Both roles were also enabled and restricted by donors and Israel. The clearance revenue mechanism dictated the PA's role within a triangle of rentier reliance whereby Israel collected and awarded rents from the business community to the PA. On the other hand, PA–business community relations were characterised by the PA's asymmetrical reliance on traders' compliance in submitting clearance receipts. In turn, the PA exploited the arrears system to co-opt some segments of the business community.

This analysis points to the PA's constant drive to exploit its rentier structure and create new mechanisms to coerce or co-opt its society. At times, the PA exercised substantial leverage over the NGO sector, but on other occasions the sector regained its independence. The PA's asymmetrical reliance on the local business community through the clearance revenue mechanism quickly transferred to demonstrable leverage through the arrears system. But if the PA consolidated its arrears debt, the asymmetrical relationship would be reinstated in favour of the local business community. Finally, the PA's defective hiring practices both encouraged voluntary co-optation and created an increasingly exclusionary government. The three cases presented provide evidence that the PA's engagement with its society was largely reduced to securing and distributing rentier income. The PA engaged in continuous rent-seeking that, in turn, hindered its capacity to craft a clearly defined rentier contract with its society. The resultant state–society relations were characterised by sustained and frequent changes in the roles and limitations of actors within the larger political economy. As long as the current rentier structure is present, competition, spontaneous and short-lived rentier contracts, and partial co-optation will continue to shape the PA's relationship with its society.

## 6.3 Thematic Considerations

Four main themes were present throughout the main arguments of the book that may have wider theoretical implications and necessitate further research. First, rentier income in the case of Palestine was not fully centralised and was channelled through mechanisms independent of the central authority. Both the broader Palestinian economy and the PA's revenues were based on remittances and aid flows, but donor preferences meant a substantial portion of foreign aid was channelled outside the PA's control, which created leverage for different actors and forces in the political economy to directly influence the state and its ability to co-opt and coerce. This manifested in the PA's constant competition with the NGO sector over donor funding. A similar phenomenon was visible in the clearance revenue mechanism, with Israel's direct interaction with Palestinian traders stripping the PA of its ability to maintain hegemony over fiscal resources and strengthening the business sector's bargaining position vis-à-vis the PA. The clearance bills system granted some traders coercive power, which, through the Large Taxpayer Unit, shaped state institutions and state–society relations.

Second, conditions imposed by rent providers meant that the PA was continually balancing two separate conditionality mechanisms. The first was a set of technical conditionalities, whereby foreign donors and Israel forced the PA to take procedural steps in order to qualify for rent disbursements. Such conditions included foreign donors' oversight of the PA's public records, and Israel's clearance bills system. The second mechanism comprised a set of political conditionalities imposed by comprehensive economic, political and security policies. Third, outward accountability and externally empowered co-optation constrained the PA.

Conditionalities and inconsistent rent disbursement altered the accountability of the PA in favour of rent providers, resulting in the weak state–society relations and a limited capacity to co-opt society. Even the PA's limited success in co-opting some segments of society was an outcome of external empowerment by rent providers rather than a result of increased domestic legitimacy. Finally, the PA's capacity was further limited by the fragmentation of governance structures. Continual competition between the PA and the NGO sector over foreign aid fragmented services provision and created parallel governance units. Internally, PA ministries competed for legitimacy with foreign donors, resulting in fragmented and overlapping decision-making governance structures. Furthermore, donor-funded units within the Ministry of Finance and Planning created resentment between public employees and unnecessarily duplicated administrative duties.

## 6.4 Towards a Fiscally Independent Palestinian State

In the Occupied Palestinian Territories, the PA is unlikely to be able to finance its operations independent of donor- or Israeli-controlled fiscal revenues. This is due to the historical and political circumstances underpinning the donor- and Israeli-engineered rentier structure of the Palestinian economy, which perpetuates the PA's dependence on foreign aid and clearance revenue. It is also due to the PA's high public expenditure and low level of domestic tax mobilisation. The question arises, then, of how an independent Palestinian state would finance its operations. Assuming that this state would be established in the West Bank and Gaza, based on or around the two-state parameters agreed upon in the Oslo process, it would have to be heavily dependent on external income in the form of remittances, foreign aid and, potentially, natural resource rents.

Palestine, along with other eastern Mediterranean states, is home to significant deposits of natural gas and oil (Khadduri 2012, pp. 112–13; Kattan 2012). The PA has approved several plans to commence operations in the natural gas fields offshore from Gaza, but Israeli restrictions have halted these developments (Palestine Investment Fund 2019). It is estimated that these natural resources would provide the PA with significant income. In addition, the declaration of an independent Palestinian state would most likely be accompanied by large foreign aid disbursements.

For example, the White House's widely criticised 'Peace to Prosperity' plan included provisions for USD 50 billion of aid and other forms of external income over a ten-year period (White House 2019). Similarly, then Vice-President John Kerry's peace initiative in 2013–2014 introduced a USD 4 billion investment incentive to the Palestinian economy and the PA (Khalidi et al. 2013).

As such, the windfall of external income in a future Palestinian state would most likely perpetuate the rentier character of the PA and the wider Palestinian economy. To avert this dynamic, the conditions that perpetuate Palestine's weak state–society relationship—including unaccountable institutions, externally empowered legitimacy and a fixation on securing external funding—must be addressed institutionally in favour of effective and accountable governance. This, in conjunction with accountable and transparent tax mobilisation efforts, may provide more conducive conditions for an independent state. In addition to institutional variables, significant investment and careful planning would be required to reverse the erosion of the Palestinian economy's productive industries, particularly in the manufacturing and agricultural sectors.

## References

Kattan, Victor. 2012. *Oil, Religion, Occupation: A Combustible Mix.* AlShabaka Policy Brief. https://al-shabaka.org/briefs/oil-religion-occupation-combustible-mix/.

Khadduri, Walid. 2012. 'East Mediterranean Gas: Opportunities and Challenges.' *Mediterranean Politics* 17, no. 1: 112–13.

Khalidi, Rashid, Diana Buttu, Raja Khalidi, Samia al-Botmeh, and Mouin Rabbani. 2013. 'Chronicles of a Death Foretold.' *Journal of Palestine Studies* 43, no. 3: 40–55.

Palestine Investment Fund. 2019. *Annual Report 2018.* http://www.pif.ps/annual-reports/.

White House. 2019. 'Peace to Prosperity.' https://www.whitehouse.gov/peacetoprosperity/.

# INDEX

**A**
Abbas, Mahmoud, 109, 110, 120
Abd al-Majid Shoman, 123
Accra Agenda for Action, 106
Afghanistan, 4, 53
Agency for Development, 108
al-Aqqad, Omar, 123
al-Masri, Bashar, 125
al-Masri, Munib, 123
Arafat, Yasser, 104, 115, 123
Arens, Moshe, 40
arrears system, 129
Automated System for Customs Data
    Analysis (ASYCUDA), 126

**B**
banking sector, 86, 88
Bishara, Shukri, 121

**C**
Canada, 73
clearance revenue, viii, 5, 6, 8–10, 15,
    29, 38, 44, 53, 57–59, 62, 65,
73, 75, 81–83, 86, 89, 90, 98,
    105, 142
suspension of, 59, 124
Coalition for Accountability and
    Integrity (AMAN), 109, 116
corporate tax, 5
corruption, 92, 116, 122, 124

**D**
de-development, 28
diaspora, 123
dual rentierism, viii, 8–10, 99, 105,
    111, 143, 145
Dutch Disease, 25, 26, 29, 72,
    76–78, 144

**E**
East Timor, 4
European Economic Community, 43
European Union, 7, 39, 73, 108, 115

**F**
Fatah, 104, 114, 116–118

© The Author(s), under exclusive license to Springer Nature
Switzerland AG 2023
A. Iqtait, *Funding and the Quest for Sovereignty in Palestine*,
https://doi.org/10.1007/978-3-031-19478-8

151

## 152 INDEX

Fayyad, Salam, 104–106, 109, 110, 115, 123, 130, 146
fiscal reform, 124
foreign aid, viii, 3, 5, 6, 8–10, 21, 22, 29, 38, 42, 43, 47, 52, 57, 59, 64, 72, 76, 81, 86, 89, 98, 105, 142
   and conditionality, 8, 23, 24, 98, 100, 108, 116, 143, 147
   definition of, 3
   impact on development, 24–26, 87

### G
Gaza, 4, 6, 9, 28, 40, 43, 49, 50, 99, 104, 117, 143, 148
General Union of Palestinian Teachers (GUPT), 117, 118, 120
General Union for Palestinian Teachers in the Occupied Territories (GUPTOT), 118, 120
Goldscheid, Rudolf, 2
government bonds, 87, 88

### H
Hamas, 50, 60, 62, 100, 104
Hamdallah, Rami, 110, 120, 121

### I
income tax, 5, 44, 46, 79, 80
informal economy, 79
International Monetary Fund, 7, 39, 57, 63, 104, 115, 121
Intifada (first), 47, 99
Intifada (second), 50, 60, 62, 104, 120, 123, 124
Iran, 17
Iraq, 4
Islamic Development Bank, 108
Israel, 7, 105, 107, 117, 120, 124, 127

   and clearance revenue, 4, 57, 59, 62, 65
   and Palestinian labour, 40, 41, 44, 47–49, 65, 74, 75, 112, 143
   impact of policies, 28, 39, 40, 46, 64, 143
   occupation, 7, 8, 10, 28, 38, 39, 44, 64, 79, 91, 98, 99, 107, 117, 143, 144
   remittances from, 5
Israeli Central Bureau of Statistics, 39

### J
Joint Jordanian-Palestinian Committee to Support the Steadfastness of the Palestinian People in the Occupied Homeland, 43
Jordan, 42, 43, 53, 63, 113

### K
Kerry, John, 149
Khoury, Said, 123
Kosovo, 4, 22

### L
labour unions, 8
Law of Public Debt in 2005, 88
Lebanon, 53, 113
legislation
   Basic Law of 1994, 113
   Charitable Associations and Community Organisations Law, 102, 107, 109
   Civil Service Law, 115, 119
   Income Tax Law Number 8, 80
   Law of Public Debt in 2005, 88

### M
Marshall Plan, 3

migration, 41
Millennium Development Goals, 3
monopolies, 124

**N**
national accounts, 42, 89
neopatrimonialism, 27
NGO Development Center, 108
NGO sector, 98, 99, 101–110, 113,
    122, 130, 145–147
  NGO Trust Fund, 102
  Palestinian Non-Governmental
    Organisations Network
    (PNGO), 103
  Union of Charitable Associations,
    103

**O**
Oman, 63
Oslo Accords, 47, 50, 72, 73, 75,
    101, 104, 113, 143, 144, 148

**P**
Palestine, 4
  business community, 8, 10, 79, 82,
    84, 86, 92, 98, 122–124, 126,
    145–147
  civil society, 8, 10
  labour market, 41, 50, 63, 75, 78,
    112
  public sector employment, 50, 62,
    63, 99, 111–114, 121, 145
  security apparatus, 8
  security sector, 63, 113–115, 120
  standards of living, 76, 78
  tourism, 73
  trade, 73, 74, 82, 83, 90–92, 127,
    145, 147
Palestine Centre for Policy and Survey
  Research, 121

Palestinian Authority, 4–8, 10, 15,
    24, 26, 27, 29, 40, 47, 48, 53,
    65, 100, 103, 106, 109, 110,
    121, 122, 142
  debt, 86, 88
  Directorate of International
    Relations and Projects, 81
  Large Taxpayer Unit, 126–128, 147
  Ministry of Education and Higher
    Education, 119, 120
  Ministry of Finance and Planning,
    39, 80, 81, 91, 92, 115, 123,
    124, 126, 129
  Ministry of Interior, 102, 110, 115
  Ministry of Justice, 103
  Ministry of National Economy, 39,
    110
  Ministry of NGOs Affairs, 102
  Ministry of Planning and
    International Cooperation, 104
  revenues, 53, 57–59, 62, 65, 72,
    75, 79, 80, 85, 86, 90, 92,
    105, 126, 142, 144
Palestinian Central Bureau of
  Statistics, 107
Palestinian Economic Council for
  Development and Reconstruction
  (PECDAR), 104
Palestinian–Israeli conflict, 9
Palestinian Legislative Council, 62,
  117, 119
Palestinian Liberation Organization,
  4, 27, 43, 46, 73, 113, 114, 117,
  119
Paris Declaration on Aid Effectiveness,
  23, 106
Paris Protocol, 4, 5, 72–74, 76, 78,
  85, 91, 123, 144
poverty, 78

**Q**
Qatar, 53

154 INDEX

**R**
Rawabi, 125
remittances, 9, 38, 40, 42, 47, 48, 72, 76, 89, 143
rentier effect, 20, 62, 64, 91
rentier income, 2, 3, 10, 38, 58, 62, 65, 89
  definition of, 16
  impacts of, 19, 76, 98, 114, 143, 144
  natural resource rents, 3, 10, 21, 23–25, 143, 148
  political rents, 3, 8–10, 21–25, 142, 143
rentier paradox. *See* rentier trap
rentier state theory, 3, 8, 9, 16–19, 21, 22, 27, 29, 142
rentier trap, 10, 78, 89, 98, 144
repression effect, 20
Rome Statute of the International Criminal Court, 60

**S**
Sadan Committee, 40
Saudi Arabia, 53, 63
Schumpeter, Joseph, 1, 2, 16, 17
Separation Wall, 50
Shihada, Jamil, 118
Shoman, Abd al-Majid, 123
Shtayyeh, Mohammad, 110
state–society relations, viii, 3, 6, 8, 9, 19, 20, 24, 27–29, 92, 98, 142, 143, 147, 148
Suhwail, Ahmad, 120

Suwan, Muhammad, 118

**T**
tax evasion, 79, 80, 88, 92
teacher strikes, 117–121, 146
transparency, 98, 116, 124, 143
Tunisia, 113, 117
Turkey, 73

**U**
unemployment, 112
unionisation, 117
United Nations, 3, 4, 43, 49, 57, 59, 60, 102, 115
  Development Program (UNDA), 43
  Educational, Scientific and Cultural Organization (UNESCO), 60
  Relief and Works Agency (UNRWA), 43, 58, 89
United States, 7, 43, 59, 73, 149
United States Agency for International Development (USAID), 39, 43, 89, 107

**W**
Weber, Max, 2
West Bank, 4, 6, 9, 28, 41, 43, 49, 50, 99, 104, 117, 120, 143
World Bank, 7, 38, 39, 51, 52, 57, 63, 78, 83, 85, 88, 101–105, 108, 115, 116, 119, 121